Praise for

DOPAMINE NATION

"Explore[s] the dichotomy between seeking a readily accessible hit of dopamine—from our phones, gambling, or a bag of Fritos—and maintaining healthy, productive, stable lives."

—*The New York Times*, Inside the Bestseller List

"[An] eye-opening survey on pleasure-seeking and addiction . . . Readers looking for balance will return to Lembke's informative and fascinating guidance." —*Publishers Weekly* (starred review)

"Fascinating case histories, and a sensible formula for treatment."

—*Kirkus Reviews*

"Anna Lembke deeply understands an experience I hear about often in the therapy room at the nexus between our modern addictions and our primal brains. Her stories of guiding people to find a healthy balance between pleasure and pain have the power to transform your life."

—Lori Gottlieb, "Dear Therapist" columnist at *The Atlantic*, *New York Times* bestselling author of *Maybe You Should Talk to Someone*

"Just when you thought you knew all you needed to know about the addiction crisis, along comes Dr. Anna Lembke with her second brilliant book on the topic—this one not about a drug but about the most powerful chemical of all: the dopamine that rules the pain and pleasure centers of our minds. In an era of overconsumption and instant gratification, *Dopamine Nation* explains the personal and societal price of being ruled by the next fix—and how to manage it. No matter what you might find yourself overindulging in—from the internet to food to work to sex—you'll find this book riveting, scary, cogent, and cleverly argued. Lembke weaves patient stories with research in a voice that's as empathetic as it is clear-eyed."

—Beth Macy, author of *Washington Post* Best Book of the Year and
New York Times Notable Book of 2018 and bestseller *Dopesick: Dealers, Doctors, and the Drug Company That Addicted America*

"We all desire a break from our routines and those parts of life that upset us. What if, instead of trying to escape these things, we learn to turn toward them, to reach a peaceful harmony with ourselves and the people we share our lives with? Lembke has written a book that radically changes the way we think about mental illness, pleasure, pain, reward, and stress. Turn toward it. You'll be happy you did."

—Daniel Levitin, *New York Times* bestselling author of
The Organized Mind and *Successful Aging*

ALSO BY ANNA LEMBKE

Dopamine Nation
Drug Dealer, MD

THE OFFICIAL

DOPAMINE NATION

WORKBOOK

A Practical Guide to Overcoming Addiction in the
Age of Indulgence

DR ANNA LEMBKE

HEADLINE PRESS

First published in the USA in 2024 by Dutton
An imprint of Penguin Random House LLC

First published in the UK in 2024 by Headline Press
An imprint of Headline Publishing Group.

4

Book design by Alison Cnockaert

Cataloguing in Publication Data is available from the British Library

Trade Paperback ISBN 978 1 0354 1655 4

Offset in 10.8/19.2pt Freight Text Pro Book by Jouve (UK), Milton Keynes

Printed and bound in Great Britain by Clays Ltd, Elcograf S.p.A.

Headline's policy is to use papers that are natural, renewable and recyclable
products and made from wood grown in well-managed forests and other
controlled sources. The logging and manufacturing processes are expected to
conform to the environmental regulations of the country of origin.

Headline Publishing Group
An Hachette UK Company
Carmelite House
50 Victoria Embankment
London EC4Y 0DZ

The authorised representative in the EEA is Hachette Ireland, 8 Castlecourt
Centre, Dublin 15, D15 XTP3, Ireland (email: info@hbgi.ie)

www.headline.co.uk
www.hachette.co.uk

This book aims to provide useful information that serves as a starting point but is not
intended to replace the diagnostic expertise and medical advice of your doctor. Please
consult with your doctor before making any health decisions, particularly if you believe
you have any medical conditions that may require treatment. The publisher and author
specifically disclaim responsibility for any loss or damage that may result from the use of
information contained in this book.

Some names and identifying details of certain people mentioned
in this book have been changed.

For my patients, who continue to inspire me every day.

CONTENTS

THE OFFICIAL

DOPAMINE
NATION

WORKBOOK

INTRODUCTION

I wrote this workbook as a companion to *Dopamine Nation* for individuals, parents, families, counselors, therapists, teachers, and others who want to go beyond narrative and engage in practices that will reset reward pathways for a more flourishing life. If that's you, then I'm so excited for the journey we're about to take together.

As in *Dopamine Nation*, the big idea in this book is that abundance itself is a stressor, contributing to rising rates of addiction, depression, anxiety, and suicide all over the world. More humans than ever before have their basic survival needs met (food, clothing, shelter). We also have more disposable income, more access to luxury goods, and more leisure time than at any point in human history, even among the poorest of the poor. (By 2040, the number of leisure hours in a typical day in the United States is projected to be 7.2 hours, with just 3.8 hours of daily work.) Almost every aspect of human life has been engineered to be more positively reinforcing, more accessible, more novel, and more potent . . . in other words, *addictive*.

Yet according to survey reports, people are less happy, more depressed, and more anxious today than they were thirty years ago. They're also dying younger. Seventy percent of global deaths today are related to modifiable risk factors such as smoking, physical inactivity, and poor diet. Most perplexing of all, the richer the country and the more access to mental health treatment, the unhappier, more depressed, and more anxious its people are, a phenomenon I call the *Plenty Paradox*.

In addition to the stress of overabundance, I suspect we're getting something fundamentally wrong about mental health. Over the course of my career as a psychiatrist, I have seen more and more patients, including otherwise healthy young people with loving families, elite education, and relative wealth, who suffer from life-shattering depression and anxiety. Their problem isn't trauma, social dislocation, or poverty. It's overabundance, and the way that constant exposure to quick pleasures changes our brains.

A patient of mine, Justin, a bright and thoughtful young man in his early twenties, came to see me for debilitating anxiety and depression. Having dropped out of college, he was living with his parents and vaguely contemplating suicide. He was also playing video games most of every day and late into every night.

Twenty years ago the first thing I would have done for a patient like this would have been to prescribe an antidepressant. Today I recommended something altogether different: a dopamine fast. I suggested he abstain from all video games for one month.

"Whaaaat?" he said. "Why would I do that?! Playing video games is the only thing that gives me any relief."

As I explained to this patient, when we do something we enjoy—like playing video games—the brain releases a little bit of dopamine, our reward neurotransmitter, and we feel good. But one of the most important discoveries in the field of neuroscience in the past seventy-five years is that pleasure and pain are processed in the same parts of the brain. The brain tries hard to keep them in balance. Whenever the balance tips in one direction, our brains work to restore neutrality, which neuroscientists call *homeostasis*, by tipping in the other direction.

As soon as dopamine is released, the brain adapts to increased dopamine by reducing or "downregulating" the number of dopamine receptors stimulated. This causes the brain to level out by tipping to the side of pain, which is why pleasure is usually followed by a feeling of hangover or comedown. If we can wait long enough, that feeling passes and neutrality is restored. But there's a natural tendency to counteract it by going back to the source of pleasure for another dose.

If we maintain this pattern for hours every day, over weeks or months, the brain's set point for pleasure changes. Now we need to keep playing games, not to feel pleasure but just to feel normal. As soon as we stop, we experience the universal symptoms of withdrawal from any addictive substance: anxiety, irritability, insomnia, dysphoria, and mental preoccupation with using, otherwise known as *craving*.

In sum, the relentless pursuit of pleasure can lead to *anhedonia*, the inability to experience any pleasure at all. Whereas by abstaining from pleasurable substances and/or behaviors for a period of time, we reset our reward pathways and recapture our capacity for joy.

My patient was convinced enough to give it a try.

He came back a month after having abstained from video games, reporting feeling better than he had in years. Less anxious. Less depressed. Why? Because when he stopped bombarding his reward pathways with dopamine, he gave his brain the opportunity to restore baseline levels of dopamine firing. He was more surprised than anyone that he felt better, which is common. It's hard to see cause and effect when we're chasing dopamine. It's only after we've taken a break from our drug of choice that we're able to see the true impact of our consumption on our lives and the people around us.

But let's not pretend that this process is easy. Far from it. Depending on the drug, the person, and the circumstances, it can feel like climbing Mount Everest in a bathing suit. So we have to plan for it, take it one step at a time, and get support from other people.

Further, the problem of our addictogenic ecosystem (a world in which everything has been druggified) is a collective one. The corporations that produce and profit from these potent pleasure goods we consume are also responsible for helping to find solutions. Schools, governments, and other large institutions can and should create guardrails and incentives to shape healthy behavior. But we as individuals and individual families can't wait for them to take action. Lives are at stake. We need to start wherever we are, right now, and do what we can. By changing ourselves, one person at a time, we can also change the world.

The acronym DOPAMINE, as described in *Dopamine Nation*, provides the structural framework for the interactive road map that follows. Each chapter is dedicated to a different letter in the acronym: Data, Objectives, Problems, Abstinence and Asceticism, Mindfulness, Insight (and Radical Honesty),

Next Steps, and Experiment. The goal of *The Official Dopamine Nation Workbook* is to provide a scalable resource to help everyday people better navigate a pathological pleasure/pain environment.

D = Data

O = Objectives

P = Problems

A = Abstinence and Asceticism

M = Mindfulness

I = Insight (and Radical Honesty)

N = Next Steps

E = Experiment

HOW TO USE THIS WORKBOOK

There is no one right way to use this workbook. You could read through the whole thing first and then go back and do the exercises. You could go directly to those chapters that are most relevant to you and then circle back to the ones you missed. But to get the most out of this book, and to optimize your chances of successful and lasting behavior change, I recommend that you go through the workbook in the following way:

- Read through and complete the exercises in chapters 1 through 4 *before* beginning the dopamine fast described in chapter 4.

- During the dopamine fast, complete chapters 5 and 6.

- As you near the end of the dopamine fast, complete chapters 7 and 8.

However you decide to engage with this workbook, the key is that you *are* engaging. Get out your pens, pencils, highlighters, markers, and maybe even crayons and write in this thing. Muck it up. Jot down your thoughts and ideas. Tear out key pages and stuff them in your pocket and planner and bring them with you to read on the train, at your desk at work, or stopped at a traffic light. The process may be sacred, but the workbook shouldn't be. Write in it and make it yours, my friend.

If you're someone who would rather adapt these pages to a digital medium, be my guest. Working with a lot of engineering types in Silicon Valley, I have many patients who make their own amazing spreadsheets from the suggested exercises herein. But if you, like me, are struggling to create more time away from screens, then I encourage you to stick with the slower, more tactile experience of writing in the book.

Finally, there's no specified timeline for how long it should take you to finish any part of this workbook. Do it at your own pace. But remember that the perfect is the enemy of the good, and that it's better to get it done than to do half of it perfectly and never finish. Also, in general, I suggest that as you're doing the exercises, write down just enough so it makes sense to you. Don't feel the need to write in complete sentences or be grammatically correct or particularly legible. The important things are that you're interacting with the ideas and organizing your responses into a coherent enough whole to get through the workbook.

So let's get started. There's no time to waste. This is your life we're talking about.

CHAPTER 1

Data

D = Data

O = Objectives

P = Problems

A = Abstinence and Asceticism

M = Mindfulness

I = Insight (and Radical Honesty)

N = Next Steps

E = Experiment

The *D* in DOPAMINE stands for *data*. We're focused here on facts, not feelings. Not that feelings are unimportant. Far from it. But feelings come later.

Addiction broadly defined is the continued, compulsive use of a substance or behavior despite harm to self and/or others. Addiction occurs on a spectrum. Most of us are not dealing with life-threatening addictions, but nearly all of us are struggling with some form of compulsive overconsumption.

To begin, think of a substance or behavior—perhaps there's more than one—that you are using in ways contrary to your desires or intentions, or that produces effects that run counter to your goals and expectations for your health, relationships, or career. Perhaps you're using more than you planned. Perhaps you've repeatedly told yourself, *Tomorrow I'm going to take a break*, but then tomorrow never comes. Perhaps you're lying about your use, minimizing the time and money spent. Perhaps other people have commented that you're using too much.

Go beyond the kinds of substances and behaviors we traditionally think of as addictive, like alcohol and cigarettes. Widen your lens to appreciate that in today's world, we can get addicted to almost anything, because almost everything has been engineered to be more reinforcing, novel, plentiful, and accessible. Consider processed food, social media, video games, online shopping, exercise, texting . . . the list really is endless. As discussed in *Dopamine Nation*, in my early forties I developed a mild addiction to reading risqué romance novels.

People can get addicted to aversive or painful stimuli as much as to pleasurable ones. For example, I struggle with obsessive ruminations about my kids' well-being. *Rumination*, derived from the Latin verb *rūmināre*, "to chew the cud," means to turn things over and over again in our minds. I can spend hours a day on unproductive worry about my children, causing harm to me and them. It causes harm to me because I waste precious time thinking about things over which I have little or no control, instead of contemplating problems in the here and now that I can actually do something about. It causes harm to my children because it objectifies them, turning their well-being into my well-being in a codependent cycle that puts pressure on them to be well, or at least to appear well, even when they aren't. In a weird way, worrying is my *happy place*.

My patients have described similar obsessive, undirected worrying about national politics, global warming, getting ill, past traumas, making mistakes, and so on.

You might well ask, *What is the difference between a passion, a habit, and an addiction?* The crucial difference is whether the substance or behavior is causing harm. The harm is not always immediately apparent, either because we can't see it even when others can or because the harm is subtle and cumulative. When it comes to drugs we are taking as medicine and/or sub-stances and behaviors that are culturally celebrated, like work, prestige, money, and power, harms are notoriously hard to detect.

Even if you don't think you have a major problem with overconsuming certain behaviors or substances, perhaps there are areas where you have to regularly work to keep things in check, or they could become unbalanced and cause harm in your life.

———

See the table on the next page, listing substances and behaviors my patients and readers, and I myself, have experienced an unhealthy relationship with over the years, including drugs, medications, media, the Internet, technol-ogy, other people, our own bodies, sports, exercise, games, adrenaline, food, work, achievement, and money.

Circle the substances and/or behaviors that you've struggled with at some point in your life, past or present, especially those behaviors you'd like to change, or you're contemplating changing. Don't gloss over this step. It's essential to slow it down and take the time to really look at our behaviors. Focusing our attention in this way increases awareness. Awareness is the first step toward change.

INTERACTIVE EXERCISE:
Identifying Problematic Substances and Behaviors
(Circle the compulsive behaviors that apply to you.)

Drugs	Medications	Media, internet, technology	Other people, our own bodies	Sports, exercise, games, adrenaline	Food	Work, achievement, money
Alcohol	Opioids	Watching videos, movies, shows	Love	Video games	Sugar	Work obsession
Nicotine	Sedatives	Social media, texting, posting, blogging, liking, commenting	Sex	Playing sports, endurance training, exercising despite worsening an injury	Caffeine, energy drinks	Winning awards, public recognition
Cannabis	Stimulants	Endless mindless scrolling	Pornography, dating apps	Watching sports	Sodas	Public speaking
Heroin	Antidepressants and mood stabilizers	Doomscrolling, online news, commentary	Masturbation	Sports betting	Fat	Social media followers/likes
Hallucinogens	Muscle relaxants	Celebrity gossip	Self-cutting	Playing chess, playing cards	Salt	Adulation, compliments
Inhalants	Cough and cold medicines	Online sports	Hair pulling	Slot machines, lotteries, scratchers	Carbohydrates/ starches	Investing, stock trading, checking investments
Cocaine	Headache medicines	Online medical information	Tattoos	Stealing, starting fires	Ultra-processed foods	Bonuses
Meth	Sleep medicines	Online travel information	Manipulating other people	Skydiving, bungee jumping, rock climbing	Bingeing	Cryptocurrency
Psychedelics	Supplements	Online weather information	Lying	Cars, motorcycles, speeding, off-roading	Binge-purging	Material acquisition to signal wealth: cars, clothes, house, watches, jewelry
Kratom	Steroids	Online shopping	Worrying	Getting in fights, rage attacks, physical violence	Restricting, calorie counting	Moving up in the professional hierarchy: corporate, legal, academic, military

For example, my problematic use tends to center around escapist fiction, mindless YouTube videos, chocolate, and worrying about my kids. My patient Riley* is struggling with Netflix, TikTok, alcohol, and overeating processed food. My patient Andy, by contrast, has a problem with excessive exercise and restricting his diet through obsessive calorie counting. How about you?

Take the substances or behaviors you circled in the table above, or any additional ones you didn't find in the table that you've added, and transpose them onto the table below, putting a check or an X in the columns that apply to that particular behavior. This exercise will help you better characterize your behavior, including use that is out of control, that involves lying to cover up the behavior, and that has been noticed by others.

---

* To respect their privacy and with their consent, names and other identifying information have been changed, including "Riley" and "Andy."

ANNA LEMBKE

INTERACTIVE EXERCISE:
Characterizing Problematic Substances and Behaviors

Substance or behavior	Using more of, or more often, than I had planned	Tried to cut back but then couldn't, or came up with an excuse to keep using	Lied about using or reported using less of, or less often, than I really did to myself or others	Other people commented on or expressed concern about my behavior

———

Having identified our problematic behaviors, let's focus now on frequency and quantity. Frequency and quantity are important because we naturally tend to minimize our use, and because the more of a drug or behavior we engage with, the more we change our brains and risk getting caught in the vortex of addiction.

By using the objective information we have at hand, and breaking down our consumption into twenty-four-hour chunks over the past week, rather than estimating our average over the week, we are much more likely to get an accurate accounting. Charting day-by-day consumption over one week is the Time-Line-Follow-Back Method, which has proven to be a more accurate way of measuring alcohol consumption than asking, "How much do you drink in a given week?" We use this approach in clinical care for all substances and behaviors.

How does improved awareness enhance agency? It may have something to do with the prefrontal cortex. The prefrontal cortex is the large gray-matter area behind our foreheads that is activated when we're telling stories, appreciating future consequences, and delaying gratification. It's also a key part of our brain's reward circuitry, serving as the brakes on overconsumption. See the simplified image of the brain's reward pathways on the next page, consisting of the prefrontal cortex, the nucleus accumbens, and the ventral tegmental area.

DOPAMINE REWARD PATHWAYS
IN THE BRAIN

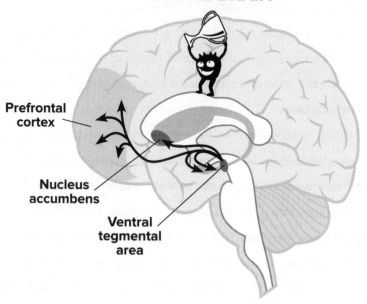

Prefrontal cortex

Nucleus accumbens

Ventral tegmental area

Our self-stories not only shape past experience; they also provide road maps for the future. When we're accurately observing and narrating our behavior, we have access to better information than if the behaviors are simply pinging around in the dark recesses of our minds. We're also creating cognitive dissonance—lack of fit with our outdated mind models—which in turn leads us to create newer, better models to fit how the world really works, or our best approximation thereof.

———

Think about the past week. How much and how often have you used your drug of choice? I use the term *drug* here to encompass both substances we ingest and behaviors we enact.

If it's a digital behavior, your device may have objective data on your app. Use it. We have a tendency to avoid looking at our digital data because it tells a different story than the one we've got going in our heads. But getting accurate data is critical, so look at those digital numbers and tally them below.

For example, Riley noted watching Netflix and/or TikTok nearly every day. Riley used a digital app to track these numbers. Riley was also surprised to discover consuming a total of sixteen drinks in one week. The recommended amount for an adult is no more than one drink per day for women (seven total in a week) and no more than two drinks per day for men (fourteen total in a week). By either standard, Riley was in the unhealthy range. The healthiest people on the planet drink no more than one to two standard drinks *per week*.

ANNA LEMBKE

INTERACTIVE EXERCISE:

Quantifying Use Over One Week

(Example: Riley)

Substance or behavior	MON	TUE	WED	THU	FRI	SAT	SUN	Week total
Netflix		66m		57m		34m	37m	3h 14m
TikTok	105m		17m	40m		26m	54m	4h 2m
Alcohol		2 drinks	2 drinks	2 drinks	3 drinks	4 drinks	3 drinks	16 drinks

It's your turn. Fill in the table below, recording quantity and frequency of use for each day of the past week. Try to be as specific and accurate as possible. Don't minimize.

Quantifying Use Over One Week

Substance or behavior	MON	TUE	WED	THU	FRI	SAT	SUN	Week total

There, you did it. You wrote it down. You got it out. It can be painful to focus on these numbers, but it's essential for increasing awareness. When we use language and numbers accurately to describe our behavior, we can *see* it in ways we honestly can't otherwise. Once we *see* the behavior, we can do something about it.

———

Now it's time to contextualize our behaviors within the autobiographical narratives of our lives by filling out a Lifetime Dopamine Chart. By reflecting on our bchaviors/habits/addictions in the broader context of our lived experience, we may appreciate for the first time just how long we've been engaging in these behaviors, as well as come to understand the environmental factors that have contributed to our behaviors.

Contrary to popular opinion, compulsive overconsumption doesn't always occur during stressful times. It depends on the person and their unique wiring. Some people consume more when they're stressed. Others consume more when things are going well. I happen to be in the "when things are going well" category. When I'm stressed and my adrenaline kicks in, I go into battle mode, eat less, and play less. When things are good, I'm vulnerable to letting it all hang out. My compulsive reading of romance novels began when the acute stress of raising small children was coming to an end.

Take a look at Andy's Lifetime Dopamine Chart. His compulsive behaviors related to exercise and food began around age sixteen, when a sports injury sidelined him from playing on his high school tennis team and he turned to other forms of exercise and restrictive eating to cope. That pattern continued throughout his life, but got especially bad between ages thirty-one and forty-four, while struggling through an unhappy marriage that ended in divorce. Part of his motivation to change came from being in a supportive relationship with his girlfriend and wanting to be a better father to his daughter.

INTERACTIVE EXERCISE:

Lifetime Dopamine Chart

(Draw a horizontal line from the age the activity started until it ended, or until the present day if it's ongoing.)

(Example: Andy)

Sports, exercise, games, adrenaline	Age																										
	3	4	5	6	7	8	9	10	11	12	13	14	15	16	17	18	19	20	21	22	23	24	25	26	27	28	29
Playing sports, endurance training, exercising despite worsening an injury										Sports injury, quit the team, out by myself in the gym, first started getting obsessed with fitness and appearance			working		Moved East for college; homesickness, using excessive workouts as a coping strategy			law school: compulsive exercise continues				Federal clerking	Birth of daughter; star law firm; conflict with w amt of time spent exer			

Your turn. On the table on page 18, draw a horizontal line from left to right, from the age you started your maladaptive consumptive behaviors to the age you ended them, or up until the present day if it's still active.

4	35	36	37	38	39	40	41	42	43	44	45	46	47	48	49	50	51	52	53	54	55	56	57	58	59	60	61	62	63	64	65	66	67	68	69	70

Met
girlfriend

Shoulder surgeries to repair
injuries caused by excessive exercise

from wife, in part due to
ulsive behaviors; spike in
exercise after the divorce

Engaged, start to try to
reduce compulsive behaviors

INTERACTIVE EXERCISE:

Lifetime Dopamine Chart

(Draw a horizontal line from the age the activity started until it ended, or until the present day if it's ongoing.)

	Age																										
Drugs	3	4	5	6	7	8	9	10	11	12	13	14	15	16	17	18	19	20	21	22	23	24	25	26	27	28	2
Alcohol																											
Nicotine																											
Cannabis																											
Heroin																											
Hallucinogens																											
Inhalants																											
Cocaine																											
Meth																											
Psychedelics																											
Kratom																											
Medications	3	4	5	6	7	8	9	10	11	12	13	14	15	16	17	18	19	20	21	22	23	24	25	26	27	28	2
Opioids																											
Sedatives																											
Stimulants																											
Antidepressants and mood stabilizers																											
Muscle relaxants																											
Cough and cold medicines																											
Headache medicines																											
Sleep medicines																											
Supplements																											
Steroids																											
Media, internet, technology	3	4	5	6	7	8	9	10	11	12	13	14	15	16	17	18	19	20	21	22	23	24	25	26	27	28	2
Watching videos, movies, shows																											
Social media, texting, posting, blogging, liking, commenting																											
Endless mindless scrolling																											
Doomscrolling, online news, commentary																											
Celebrity gossip																											
Online sports																											
Online medical information																											
Online travel information																											
Online weather information																											
Online shopping																											

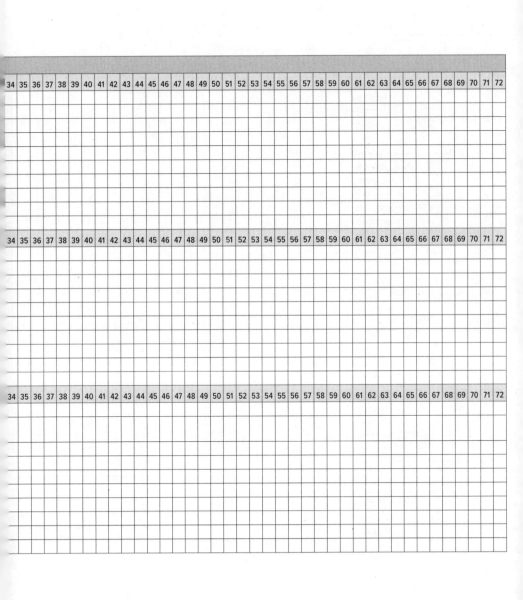

34	35	36	37	38	39	40	41	42	43	44	45	46	47	48	49	50	51	52	53	54	55	56	57	58	59	60	61	62	63	64	65	66	67	68	69	70	71	72

34	35	36	37	38	39	40	41	42	43	44	45	46	47	48	49	50	51	52	53	54	55	56	57	58	59	60	61	62	63	64	65	66	67	68	69	70	71	72

34	35	36	37	38	39	40	41	42	43	44	45	46	47	48	49	50	51	52	53	54	55	56	57	58	59	60	61	62	63	64	65	66	67	68	69	70	71	72

Other people, our own bodies	3	4	5	6	7	8	9	10	11	12	13	14	15	16	17	18	19	20	21	22	23	24	25	26	27	28	29
Love																											
Sex																											
Pornography, dating apps																											
Masturbation																											
Self-cutting																											
Hair pulling																											
Tattoos																											
Manipulating other people																											
Lying																											
Worrying																											
Sports, exercise, games, adrenaline	3	4	5	6	7	8	9	10	11	12	13	14	15	16	17	18	19	20	21	22	23	24	25	26	27	28	29
Video games																											
Playing sports, endurance training, exercising despite worsening an injury																											
Watching sports																											
Sports betting																											
Playing chess, playing cards																											
Slot machines, lotteries, scratchers																											
Stealing, starting fires																											
Skydiving, bungee jumping, rock climbing																											
Cars, motorcycles, speeding, off-roading																											
Getting in fights, rage attacks, physical violence																											
Food	3	4	5	6	7	8	9	10	11	12	13	14	15	16	17	18	19	20	21	22	23	24	25	26	27	28	29
Sugar																											
Caffeine, energy drinks																											
Sodas																											
Fat																											
Salt																											
Carbohydrates/starches																											
Ultra-processed foods																											
Bingeing																											
Binge-purging																											
Restricting, calorie counting																											
Work, achievement, money	3	4	5	6	7	8	9	10	11	12	13	14	15	16	17	18	19	20	21	22	23	24	25	26	27	28	29
Work obsession																											
Winning awards / public recognition																											
Public speaking																											
Social media followers/likes																											
Adulation, compliments																											
Investing, stock trading, checking investments																											
Bonuses																											
Cryptocurrency																											
Material acquisition to signal wealth: cars, clothes, houses, watches, jewelry																											
Moving up in the professional hierarchy: corporate, legal, academic, military																											

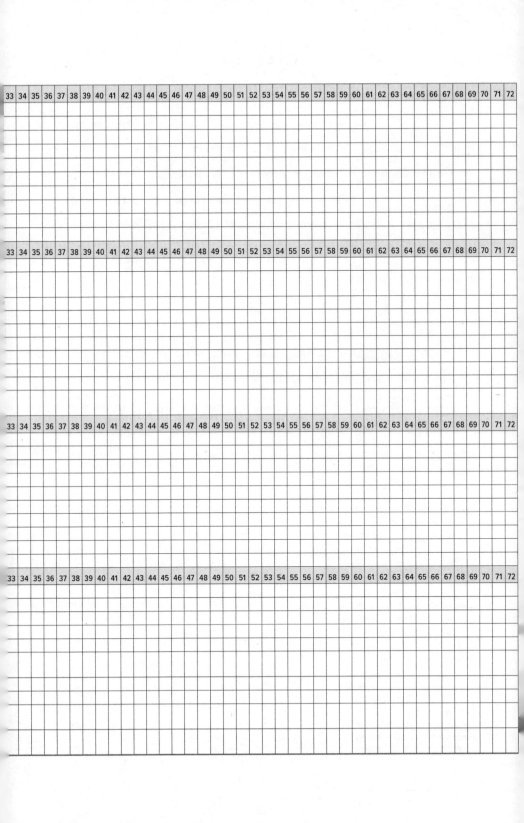

Make a notation on the same table to indicate especially painful or difficult periods or events in your life, as well as especially happy ones, that made your consumptive behaviors better or worse. Do you see any patterns? Are you someone who tends to consume in maladaptive ways when things are going well in your life and the pressure has eased off, or when things are not going well and the pressure increases? If you've had periods of abstinence or healthy moderation, what were the secret ingredients?

———

It's often only by taking the long view—either projecting ourselves forward into the future and imagining what we want to be doing at some future point, or projecting ourselves into the past and thinking about what we have lost because of all the time we spent using our drug of choice, sometimes referred to as *opportunity costs*—that we can come to appreciate these subtle, cumulative harms. The regret principle* is one way to reflect on opportunity costs: Ask yourself, "Upon sober reflection at the end of the day or the week, looking back, where did I regret spending my time?"

---

* Thanks to my colleague Steven Michael Crane for this idea.

INTERACTIVE EXERCISE:
The Regret Principle
(Example: Andy)

I regret the time I've spent on compulsive overexercising and restricting my diet, the likely permanent physical injuries that I've caused myself, and the unhealthy modeling I've provided my daughter. I also regret the feelings of shame and despair that I've caused myself with my addictive behaviors. I isolate myself from good, caring friends. I also hurt my ex-wife by making her think that my workout routine was much more important to me than she was. It was a constant point of friction and bad feelings in our relationship.

Take a few minutes to write about your reasons for regretting certain patterns of consumptive behaviors in terms of harm to self and others. Regret is a painful emotion, but an emotion full of important information that can help motivate change.

INTERACTIVE EXERCISE:

The Regret Principle

_____

_____

_____

_____

_____

_____

_____

_____

_____

_____

_____

_____

_____

_____

_____

_____

_____

_____

_____

_____

_____

_____

_____

———

We've come to the end of our chapter on "*D* is for *data*." Nice work! Let's take a moment to summarize what we've done so far.

Recap

- We've considered the wide range of substances and behaviors it is possible to use too much of and too often in our modern, druggified world.
- We've learned about the role of the prefrontal cortex in enhancing awareness of our actions, which in turn creates the possibility of acting differently.
- We've documented quantity and frequency over a single week.
- We've contemplated our consumptive behaviors in the context of our entire lives, looking for patterns that might indicate life experiences that contribute to or improve compulsive overuse.
- We've explored the regret principle: Upon sober reflection at the end of the day or the week, looking back, I regret spending my time on this.

It's time to move beyond simple facts and take a look at all-important feelings. In the next section, we'll explore what our brains are telling us about why we do the things we do, as well as why our feelings are not always to be trusted when it comes to compulsive overconsumption.

CHAPTER 2

Objectives

 D = Data

 O = **Objectives**

 P = Problems

 A = Abstinence and Asceticism

 M = Mindfulness

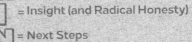 **I** = Insight (and Radical Honesty)

 N = Next Steps

 E = Experiment

The O in DOPAMINE stands for *objectives*. This is where we go beyond *what we use* and focus on *why we use*. Of note, our drug of choice is usually not accomplishing what we're hoping it will accomplish, at least not in the later stages of our use. Appreciating the gap between our objectives for using and the actual outcome requires careful analysis, which is what we'll work on now.

In my clinical and personal experience, we initiate the use of addictive substances and behaviors for one of two broad reasons: to have fun or to solve a problem. Even irrational behaviors have rational underpinnings.

See the table below for some common reasons people give for using substances and behaviors. Circle the ones that apply to you. Add others if your reasons aren't there.

Reasons for Compulsive Overconsumption

(Circle the reasons that apply to you.)

To have fun, entertain, recreate	To increase sociability	To fit in (peer pressure and perception of organizational culture)	To get attention	To stave off boredom
To improve performance	To increase productivity	To enhance concentration	To mitigate fatigue	To decrease physical pain
To treat anxiety	To treat depression	To sleep	To stop feeling, to numb, to dissociate	To feel something
To have a spiritual experience	To forget	To remember	To be more creative	To feel in control

I asked Andy, who struggles with compulsive overexercise and calorie counting, to spend some time reflecting on three reasons he engages in his addictive exercise and calorie counting.

Here's what he had to say:

INTERACTIVE EXERCISE:

Reflecting on Specific Reasons for Use

(Example: Andy)

1. _To look lean and muscular and attractive_

2. _To appear and feel tough and capable of physical feats_

3. _To cultivate a self-righteous perspective of being more hardworking and capable of enduring pain than others, including bragging to others about how hard the marathon, or other big endurance event, was_

Now I'd like you to take a few minutes to write about three of your objectives for maladaptive consumptive behaviors.

INTERACTIVE EXERCISE:

Reflecting on Specific Reasons for Use

1. _____

_____

_____

_____

_____

_____

2. _____

_____

_____

_____

_____

3. _____

_____

_____

_____

_____

_____

_____

———

By reflecting on the reasons we engage in compulsive behaviors, we can begin to explore whether our drug is accomplishing what we hoped it would
accomplish. The answers may surprise you. Oftentimes, highly reinforcing
substances and behaviors lead to the subjective feeling of having a certain
outcome but in reality don't achieve that goal. To put it another way, what
we *feel* is happening is not in fact what *is* happening.

This gap between subjective and objective reality can be difficult to
grasp unless we take the time to think about it, are radically honest with
ourselves, and accept honest feedback from others. Sometimes even then we
can't see the truth, which is why taking a break from our substance or behavior for a period of time long enough to reset reward pathways—the dopamine fast, as discussed in chapter 4—is the only way to gain insight.

In my case, I had the illusion that my obsessive worrying about my kids
made me a better mother. There was also some element of magical thinking:
I believed that by worrying about my kids, I could prevent bad things from

happening. Obviously not true, but it felt true. More important, I only realized this truth about my compulsive worrying after taking the time to think
about it.

What I discovered, after reflecting and getting honest feedback from my
children, was that when I was consumed by worry, I made *them* anxious and
was less able to be present for them in ways that were helpful for them rather
than reinforcing for me. As a result, they were less likely to share with me
what was really going on in their lives, for fear that honest disclosure would
make me worry more. Not to mention that it's no fun hanging out with
someone who is anxious all the time.

Here's a different example. A patient of mine who was a daily cannabis
smoker told me that cannabis made him more creative. I've heard this many
times over the years from many patients who use cannabis. But when he and
I together looked closer at his pot use, we realized that his *feeling* more creative didn't necessarily translate into *being* more creative. That is, he didn't
actually produce much when he was high. In fact, the work he was most
proud of occurred when he went longer stretches without using.

Next, let's try an interactive exercise to explore the gap between a desired objective and the actual outcome from substances and behaviors we're
using.

In the table on page 37, list a particular instance of use and briefly describe it. Just a shorthand description is fine, as long as it means something
to you. Then walk through the gap between what you hoped to achieve and
what really happened. What thoughts, feelings, and intentions drove use of
that substance or behavior? What was the actual outcome of using that substance or behavior? What was the gap between intention and outcome?

For example, my patient Riley wrote, "On Tuesday at home, I watched an excessive amount of YouTube videos on my phone." For thoughts, feelings, and intentions that drove use, Riley wrote, "I wanted to avoid feeling an uncomfortable feeling within me (gut/stomach) that arose from anticipating that someone I was dating wanted to stop dating." For actual outcome, Riley wrote, "Feeling of nothingness/numbness. The uncomfortable feeling within me ended up returning again." For gap between intentions and outcome, Riley wrote, "I engaged in the behavior in order to try relieving or at least avoiding the uncomfortable feeling, but it ended up coming back."

INTERACTIVE EXERCISE:
Objectives, Outcomes, and Gaps
(Example: Riley)

Specific instance of use: date, time, place, what you used	Thoughts, feelings, and intentions that drove use of the substance or behavior	Actual outcome of using the substance or behavior	Gap between intentions and outcome
On Tuesday at home, I watched an excessive amount of YouTube videos on my phone.	I wanted to avoid feeling an uncomfortable feeling within me (gut/stomach) that arose from anticipating that someone I was dating wanted to stop dating.	Feeling of nothingness/ numbness. The uncomfortable feeling within me ended up returning again.	I engaged in the behavior in order to try relieving or at least avoiding the uncomfortable feeling, but it ended up coming back.

Riley indulged in "excessive" YouTube videos to avoid feelings caused by an imminent breakup. For Riley, escaping in YouTube videos worked for a while, but ultimately the uncomfortable feelings returned. The gap? Riley's attempt to escape uncomfortable emotions led to those emotions coming back after a short period of time.

My patient Andy wrote about a unique instance of damaging his shoulder due to excessive exercise, leading to surgery to repair the damage. In the recovery phase, he overdid it again and injured another part of his body. His goal of getting stronger and chasing the feelings that come with that resulted in the opposite: a new injury and a delay in his healing process.

INTERACTIVE EXERCISE:
Objectives, Outcomes, and Gaps
(Example: Andy)

Specific instance of use: date, time, place, what you used	Thoughts, feelings, and intentions that drove use of the substance or behavior	Actual outcome of using the substance or behavior	Gap between intentions and outcome
December 15, 5:45am	My operated-on shoulder has been feeling stronger and I pushed hard to get back a feeling of control over my pre-operation level of workouts.	I pulled my hamstring and have been sore the last two days, resulting in my feeling more out of control and regretful.	I tried to assert my will to push my body to lift more weight than it was ready to lift, and ended up setting myself back and feeling more injured and foolhardy.

What about you? Use the interactive table opposite to chart the gap between your desired outcome and reality.

INTERACTIVE EXERCISE:

Objectives, Outcomes, and Gaps

Specific instance of use: date, time, place, what you used	Thoughts, feelings, and intentions that drove use of the substance or behavior	Actual outcome of using the substance or behavior	Gap between intentions and outcome

———

We've come to the end of our chapter on "O is for *objectives*." Nice work! Let's take a moment to summarize what we've done so far.

Recap

- We've considered a range of objectives for using a particular reinforcing substance or behavior.
- We've detailed *your* specific objectives for using your drug of choice and linked it to specific instances.
- We've contemplated the gap between our objectives for using and the actual outcome.

———

Next we'll explore the problems commonly associated with compulsive overuse, as well as what's happening in the brain that contributes to craving, withdrawal, and dependence.

CHAPTER 3

Problems

= Data

= Objectives

P= **Problems**

= Abstinence and Asceticism

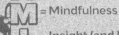= Mindfulness

= Insight (and Radical Honesty)

= Next Steps

= Experiment

The *P* in DOPAMINE stands for *problems associated with use*, especially when we use repeatedly, compulsively, and in excess. In this chapter, we will first focus on what happens in our brains when we repeatedly expose ourselves to highly reinforcing substances and behaviors, using the extended metaphor of a pleasure-pain balance to describe neuroadaptation and homeostasis. Next we'll consider the impact of chronic reinforcers, large and small, on our mental health, not just at the level of the individual but also at the level of the population and the planet, which, as referenced earlier, I've called the Plenty Paradox.

Neuroadaptation, the Pleasure-Pain Balance, and Homeostasis

Many different problems can arise from excessively indulging in substances and behaviors that are reinforcing, but chief among them may be the problem of neuroadaptation.

Neuroadaptation refers to the ways our brains change over time in response to rewarding substances and behaviors, such that they stop working or even turn on us, doing the opposite of what we expected and hoped for. So far, we've talked about this as the "gap" between desired outcome and reality. Let's look at what is going on in the brain that's causing this destructive behavior loop.

The main functional cells of the brain are called *neurons*. They communicate with each other at synapses via electrical signals and neurotransmitters. Neurotransmitters are like baseballs. The pitcher is the presynaptic neuron. The catcher is the postsynaptic neuron. The space between pitcher and catcher is the synaptic cleft. Just as the ball is thrown between pitcher and catcher, neurotransmitters bridge the distance between neurons as chemical messengers. They regulate electrical signals in the brain by making the postsynaptic neuron more or less likely to fire, which in turn affects downstream neurons.

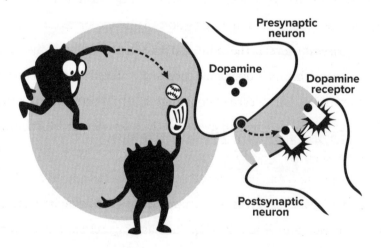

Dopamine was first identified as a human brain neurotransmitter in 1957 by two scientists working independently: Arvid Carlsson and Kathleen Montagu. The part of the brain known as the *reward pathway*, including the ventral tegmental area, the nucleus accumbens, and the prefrontal cortex, is rich in dopamine-releasing neurons. (See the image on page 10.)

Dopamine is not the only neurotransmitter involved in reward processing, but neuroscientists agree it is among the most important. Dopamine may play a bigger role in the motivation to get a reward than the pleasure of the reward itself, that is, we *want* more than we *like*. Case in point: Genetically engineered mice unable to make dopamine will chew and eat food, and seem to enjoy it, but if the same food is placed some distance away, they will starve to death. Without dopamine, they're not motivated to do the work to get the thing they need for survival.

We release dopamine in the reward pathway at a baseline rate. The deviation above and below baseline correlates with our experience of pleasure and pain. The more dopamine a substance or behavior releases, and the faster it releases dopamine, the more addictive that substance or behavior is. This is not to say that high-dopamine substances literally contain dopamine. Rather, they trigger the release of dopamine in our brain's reward pathway.

For a rat in a box, chocolate increases the basal output of dopamine in the brain by 55 percent, sex by 100 percent, nicotine by 150 percent, and cocaine by 225 percent. Amphetamine, the active ingredient in the street drugs "speed," "ice," and "shabu," as well as in medications like Adderall that are used to treat attention deficit disorder, increases the release of dopamine by 1,000 percent.

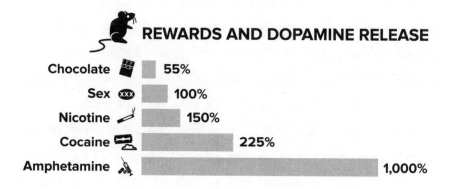

But dopamine release is not the whole story. Many different factors, such as genetics, upbringing, and environment, determine whether a person, or a rat, becomes addicted to a substance or behavior. Nonetheless, dopamine has become a kind of universal currency for measuring mechanisms of reward.

———

Let's consider what happens in the brain as people become addicted. To understand addiction, it is important to understand homeostasis. Imagine that in your reward pathway there sits a balance, like a teeter-totter in a kids' playground. In a simplified way, the balance represents how we process pleasure and pain. When the balance is at rest, it is level with the ground, or what neuroscientists call *homeostasis*.

BALANCE

PLEASURE   PAIN

When we feel pleasure, the balance tips one way. When we feel pain, it tips the other.

PLEASURE   PAIN

Several overarching rules govern this balance. First and most important, the balance wants to stay level. With any deviation from neutrality, our brains will work hard to restore a level balance. The question is how.

Our brains restore neutrality first by tipping an equal and opposite amount to whatever the initial stimulus was. I like to imagine this as these little neuroadaptation gremlins hopping on the pain side of my balance to bring it level again.

But the gremlins like it on the balance, so they don't hop off once it's level. They stay on until the balance has tipped an equal and opposite amount to the side of pain.

This is the opponent-process mechanism, otherwise known as the *hang-over, the comedown, or that moment*, sometimes just outside of conscious awareness, of wanting to consume our drug of choice one more time. The comedown is what drives the craving to reuse.

If we wait long enough without reuse, the gremlins hop off the pain side of the balance, and homeostasis is restored.

But what if we don't wait? What if instead we continue to consume our drug of choice over hours, days, weeks, months, or years? Those gremlins start to multiply, and pretty soon entire gangs of them are camped out on the pain side of the balance, moving vans and barbecues in tow.

PLEASURE   **PAIN**

We've entered addicted brain, having effectively changed our hedonic—or joy—set point to the side of pain. Now we need to use not to feel good but just to stop feeling bad. When we're not using, we are experiencing the universal symptoms of withdrawal from any addictive substance or behavior, that is, anxiety, irritability, insomnia, dysphoria, and craving. The changed hedonic set point, which neuroscientists call *allostasis*, explains in part why people relapse to their drug of choice even when they can rationally observe that their lives are better off without the drug.

Here's a graphic representation of the same concept. When we initially expose ourselves to reinforcing substances or behaviors, we feel some kind of reward as dopamine firing increases above baseline. But not long thereafter, we may experience dopamine free fall, to not just baseline but below baseline.

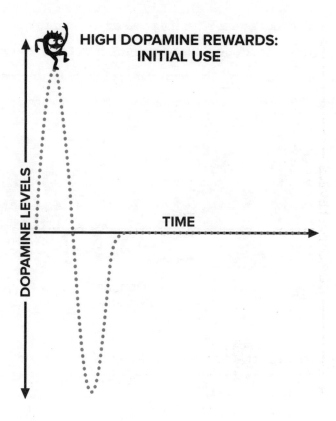

With repeated exposure over time to the same or similar reward, the initial upward deflection of dopamine gets weaker and shorter in duration, while the after-response gets stronger and longer. This may occur in part through the downregulation of postsynaptic dopamine receptors.

Now we've entered the dopamine deficit state, where we need more of our "drug" and in more potent forms to get the same effect (tolerance), and when we're not using, we're experiencing physical and psychological withdrawal that is driving reuse.

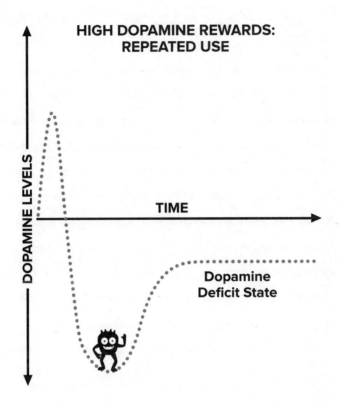

The Plenty Paradox

Before we move on to the next section, you might be asking yourself, *Why would Mother Nature create a pleasure-pain balance that requires us to experience pain in the aftermath of pleasure? Is this a cruel cosmic joke?*

Mother Nature isn't cruel, just a little behind the times. This balance is perfectly adapted to a world of scarcity and ever-present danger, which is the world humans inhabited for most of our existence. In such a world, never being satisfied with what we have and always wanting more allowed us to survive and thrive.

But here's the problem. We no longer live in that world. We've transformed the world from a place of scarcity to a place of overwhelming abundance. The access to ever-greater quantities, varieties, and potencies of highly reinforcing drugs and behaviors, including drugs that didn't exist before—texting/tweeting, vaping / video chatting, dabbing / doctor shopping—has turned us all into potential addicts. The smartphone is the equivalent of the hypodermic needle, delivering digital dopamine for a wired generation. If you haven't met your drug yet, it's coming soon to a website near you. The net effect is that we need more reward to feel pleasure, and less injury to feel pain.

As you can see in the illustration, my patient Max started at age seventeen with alcohol, cigarettes, and cannabis ("Mary Jane"). By age eighteen, he was snorting cocaine. At age nineteen, he switched to OxyContin and Xanax. Through his twenties, he used Percocet, fentanyl, ketamine, LSD, PCP, DXM, and MXE, eventually landing on Opana, a pharmaceutical-grade opioid that led him to heroin, where he stayed until he came to see me at age thirty. In total, he went through fourteen different drugs in a little over a decade.

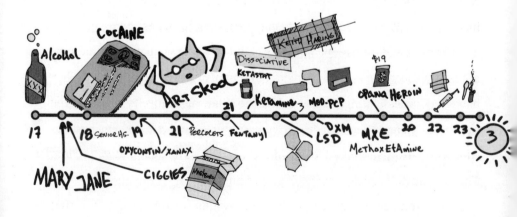

This recalibration is occurring not just at the level of the individual but also at the level of nations. Rates of happiness are going down while rates of depression, anxiety, physical pain, and suicide are going up, especially in countries with higher overall wealth.

According to the World Happiness Report, which ranks 156 countries by how happy their citizens perceive themselves to be, people living in the United States reported being less happy in 2018 than they were in 2008. Other countries with comparable measures of wealth, social support, and life expectancy saw similar decreases in self-reported happiness scores, including Belgium, Canada, Denmark, France, Japan, New Zealand, and Italy.

Researchers interviewed nearly 150,000 people in twenty-six countries to determine the prevalence of generalized anxiety disorder, defined as excessive and uncontrollable worry that adversely affects one's life. They found that high-income countries had higher rates of anxiety than low-income ones. The number of new cases of depression worldwide increased 50 percent between 1990 and 2017. The highest increases in new cases were seen in regions with the highest sociodemographic index (income), especially North America. High-income countries have higher suicide rates than low-income ones. The difference is especially striking for males.

The poor and undereducated, especially those living in wealthy nations, are most susceptible to the problem of compulsive overconsumption. They have easy access to high-reward, high-potency, high-novelty drugs at the same time that they lack access to meaningful work, safe housing, quality education, affordable health care, and race and class equality before the law. This creates a dangerous nexus of addiction risk.

Princeton economists Anne Case and Angus Deaton have shown that middle-aged white Americans without a college degree are dying younger than their parents, grandparents, and great-grandparents. The top three leading causes of death in this group are drug overdoses, alcohol-related liver disease, and suicide. Case and Deaton have aptly called this phenomenon "deaths of despair."

Our compulsive overconsumption risks not just our demise but also that of our planet. The world's natural resources are rapidly diminishing. Economists estimate that in 2040 the world's natural capital (land, forests, fisheries, fuels) will be 21 percent less in high-income countries and 17 percent less in low-income countries than today. Meanwhile, carbon emissions will grow by 7 percent in high-income countries and 44 percent in the rest of the world.

———

Okay, time to face our own gremlins. Using the table on page 56, list the substance or behavior you'd like to change and describe the problems caused by that substance or behavior in the column that corresponds to it. You'll note that the second column, "Neuroadaptation," refers to tolerance, withdrawal, and craving, or simply the gap between outcome and expectations that we've already reviewed. Other common categories of distress include relationship, work, financial, health, and value-based or spiritual problems.

For example, I've gotten into trouble with compulsively reading romance novels and codependent worrying about my kids. In both instances, I developed tolerance, needing more potent forms over time to get the same effect, and experienced problems with relationships, work, and health. With romance novels, I progressed over time from teenage vampires to reading books I was ashamed of and kept hidden. I was reading instead of spending time with family, reading instead of sleeping, and at one point even took a romance novel to work and read in the ten minutes between patients. My obsessive worrying about my kids has likewise caused significant problems, such as alienating my family with constant nagging and going against my values by reading my daughter's diary. (More later on what happens when we break trust with those we love and what to do about it.)

INTERACTIVE EXERCISE:
Exploring Problems Associated with Use
(Example: Anna)

Substance or behavior	Neuroadaptation: tolerance, withdrawal, craving	Relationship problems	Work problems	Financial problems	Health problems	Spiritual/ values problems
Reading romance novels	Needing more graphic images over time to get the same effect. Finding that I experienced less joy in other things that used to give me pleasure.	Not spending time with or being present for husband, children, friends	Started taking romance novels to work and reading between patient visits, so not focused on patients		Not getting enough sleep due to staying up late reading	Reading books that I'm ashamed to be reading and hiding from others
Worrying about my kids	Finding things to worry about even when things are going well, and feeling empty when I'm not worrying	Annoying people with my constant worrying and nagging				Reading my daughter's private journal because I was worried about her health and thought I would find the answers there

My patient Riley has struggled with overconsumption of digital media like YouTube, Netflix, podcasts, and so on, and noticed that this behavior contributed to more up-and-down moods, some inappropriate behavior with friends, procrastinating (like failing to schedule a much-needed doctor's appointment), and being less open to receiving help from others.

INTERACTIVE EXERCISE:
Exploring Problems Associated with Use

(Example: Riley)

Substance or behavior	Neuroadaptation: tolerance, withdrawal, craving	Relationship problems	Work problems	Financial problems	Health problems	Spiritual/ values problems
Digital entertainment	Life isn't in flow like it once was. Very up and down.	I am annoying to others / lack boundaries.			I neglect scheduling routine doctors' appointments and checkups.	I am trying to be the only source of solutions instead of receiving help from others.

My patient Andy, in reflecting on his exercise addiction, observed neuroadaptation as follows: "Gains in muscle and endurance plateaued and weakened. I needed to work out harder to get the same reward. I was craving the feeling of exhaustion and release after a full-out physical effort." He also noted relationship problems caused by friends and family worrying about the constant injuries, as well as work problems caused by overexercising making him late to the office. He incurred financial problems caused by significant costs from all the injuries, the gym memberships, and the therapy.

I found his description of spiritual- / values-based problems related to compulsive overexercise especially insightful: "Lying to cover up how much and how hard I'm exercising. Self-focused, narcissistic behavior. Interest in many other aspects of life falling away."

INTERACTIVE EXERCISE:
Exploring Problems Associated with Use
(Example: Andy)

Substance or behavior	Neuroadaptation: tolerance, withdrawal, craving	Relationship problems	Work problems	Financial problems	Health problems	Spiritual/values problems
Compulsive overexercise	Gains in muscle and endurance plateaued and weakened. I needed to work out harder to get the same reward. I was craving the feeling of exhaustion and release after a full-out physical effort. Needed more exercise to get the feeling. Compulsive overexercise allows me to eat a ton of food, leading to a cycle of working out more to eat more and craving more food to eat.	Friends and family concerned about me pushing body too hard to injury.	Getting to office late and exhausted from working out too long.	Gym membership money. Medical-injury costs. Therapy costs.	Physical injuries to leg and shoulder and impaired mental health.	Lying to cover up how much and how hard I'm exercising. Self-focused, narcissistic behavior. Interest in many other aspects of life falling away.

As you fill out this interactive table, remember to be as honest as you can be, but also be compassionate with yourself. Don't judge yourself or your actions. We're all caught in the vortex.

Exploring Problems Associated with Use

Substance or behavior	Neuroadaptation: tolerance, withdrawal, craving	Relationship problems	Work problems	Financial problems	Health problems	Spiritual/ values problems

We've come to the end of our chapter on "P is for *problems*." Nice work! Let's take a moment to summarize what we've done so far.

Recap

- We've considered what happens in the brain with repeated use of reinforcing substances and behaviors, namely tolerance, withdrawal, and craving. These brain changes, called *neuroadaptation*, lead to a dopamine-deficit state, a disruption of homeostasis that changes our hedonic set point such that we become more sensitive to pain and need ever more potent forms of pleasure to feel any pleasure at all.
- We've hypothesized that overabundance itself is a modern-day physiological stressor, contributing to growing unhappiness and rising rates of depression, anxiety, and suicide. We've dubbed this phenomenon the Pleasure Paradox.
- We've explored how the druggification of modern-day life especially affects poor people living in rich nations who have access to all manner of highly reinforcing substances and behaviors without comparable access to adaptive rewards like clean air, healthy food, and meaningful work.
- We've also explored how our overconsumption is harming our planet.

Now that we've finished exploring Data, Objectives, and Problems, it's time to turn our attention to what we're going to *do* about it. The best way to understand any biological system is to change one variable in that system and see what happens. Here we go.

CHAPTER 4

Abstinence and Asceticism

D = Data

O = Objectives

P = Problems

A = **Abstinence and Asceticism**

M = Mindfulness

I = Insight (and Radical Honesty)

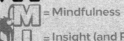**N** = Next Steps

E = Experiment

The A in DOPAMINE stands for *abstinence*, otherwise known as *dopamine fasting*. Dopamine fasting involves eliminating our substance or behavior of choice for a period of time long enough to reset reward pathways and return to healthy levels of dopamine firing. By stopping the cycle of intoxication and withdrawal, we stand a good chance of improving our mood and overall sense of well-being, taking pleasure in other, more modest rewards, and understanding the true impact of consumption on our lives.

Remember my young patient Justin, who came back a month after having abstained from video games, reporting feeling less anxious and depressed? He described being interested anew in the classes he was taking in college. By resetting his reward pathways, other activities regained their appeal, a phenomenon neuroscientists sometimes call *salience*.

But before we explore dopamine fasting, a few caveats. A dopamine fast should not be undertaken by individuals who are at risk for life-threatening withdrawal, for example, those who are severely dependent on alcohol, benzodiazepines (Xanax, Klonopin, Valium), or opioids (Norco, OxyContin, heroin), in which case please consult a professional for medically monitored withdrawal. For people with severe physiologic dependence who have altered their brains so extensively through neuroadaptation—the gremlins accumulating on the pain side of the balance—that the sudden withdrawal of their drug could lead to a physiologic storm (erratic heart rate, slowed or rapid breathing, elevated or depressed temperature, elevated or depressed blood pressure, seizures, and death), stop here and consult a medical professional.

Even in the absence of life-threatening withdrawal, some of us have become so addicted that we are unable to stop, even when we want to. Human brains can confuse the need for a drug with survival. Some will sacrifice everything they have for their drug, even at the risk of death. This is not equivalent to wanting to die. Many people with severe addiction desperately want to live. They just can't stop using. Such individuals, again, should consult a medical professional with expertise in addiction to advise them.*

With that out of the way, we're ready to get started. This chapter is longer than the others and will be divided into three parts: (1) planning for the dopamine fast; (2) self-binding; and (3) asceticism, also known as *hormesis*.

---

* In cases of severe physiologic dependence on a medication, the individual may need to taper off the medication slowly rather than abruptly discontinue it. Or they may need to take a medically sanctioned form of their drug. For example, long-acting opioids like methadone and buprenorphine are evidence-based treatments for severe opioid addiction. They work by leveling the pleasure-pain balance to relieve withdrawal and craving, so the individual can engage in other aspects of recovery. These medications can save lives and should be prescribed for appropriate individuals.

Planning for the Dopamine Fast

First, how long should we abstain from our drug of choice?

For individuals who are safely able to stop their substance or behavior, I recommend four weeks of abstinence. Why four weeks? Most people can wrap their heads around four weeks. It's not too intimidating an amount of time. Also, clinical experience dictates that it takes on average about four weeks for those neuroadaptation gremlins to hop off the pain side of the balance and for homeostasis to be restored. Less time than four weeks will result in all the pain of withdrawal without the benefits of recovery.

This is not by any means a new idea. People have known for millennia that abstaining from a substance or behavior for a period of time is salutary. It's probably no coincidence that most major religions of the world incorporate a period of fasting for approximately one month per year.

A four-week fast is also supported by scientific research. Neuroscientist Nora Volkow and her colleagues examined dopamine transmission in the brains of healthy control subjects compared to people addicted to a variety of drugs. The differences are striking. In the brain images of healthy controls, there is abundant dopamine transmission. In the brain images of people with addiction relative to healthy controls, there is little or no dopamine transmission, which can feel like clinical depression, anxiety, attention deficit disorder, or any number of aversive psychological states. Of note, these individuals gave up their drugs two weeks before the images were taken, implying that the dopamine deficit state created by heavy drug use persists at least two weeks beyond drug cessation. We don't yet have comparable brain imaging studies on when baseline healthy dopamine levels are restored, but clinical experience suggests that the most difficult time is the first ten to fourteen days after stopping, with slow but steady improvements in subjective well-being in weeks three and four.

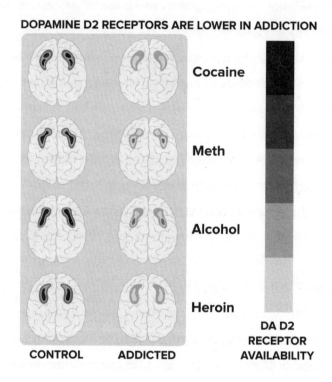

DOPAMINE D2 RECEPTORS ARE LOWER IN ADDICTION

Another experiment by psychologist Marc Schuckit and his colleagues looked at a group of men who were drinking alcohol daily in large quantities and also met criteria for clinical depression, or what is called *major depressive disorder*. The depressed men in Schuckit's study went into the hospital for four weeks, during which time they received no treatment for depression, other than stopping alcohol. After one month of not drinking, 80 percent no longer met criteria for clinical depression.

This finding implies that for the majority, clinical depression was the result of heavy drinking and not the other way around. Of course, there are other possible explanations for these results: the therapeutic milieu of the hospital environment, spontaneous remission of depression, the episodic nature of depression, which can come and go independent of external factors. But the findings are remarkable given that standard treatments for depression, whether medications or psychotherapy, have a 50 percent response rate.

These studies, along with my more than two decades of clinical experience, are consistent with a recommendation of at least four weeks of abstinence. Of course, I am not saying that addiction is cured in four weeks. But it's often only after resetting reward pathways and restoring baseline levels of dopamine transmission that the ongoing work of long-term recovery can begin.

Having done my best to persuade you to take a minimum of four weeks away from your drug of choice, I want to make it clear that if you can't do the full four weeks, even a shorter dopamine fast may be instructive. Less than four weeks probably won't be enough time to restore baseline dopamine, but it may be enough to make you realize how addicted you've become. Many patients tell me that they didn't realize they were addicted to a substance or behavior until they tried to stop and saw how difficult it was. The pain of withdrawal can sometimes provide that "Aha!" moment that creates the motivation for a longer fast.

You will know you are returning to healthier levels of dopamine firing when the universal symptoms of withdrawal—anxiety, irritability, insomnia, depression, and craving—begin to lessen. You will then be able to take pleasure in more modest rewards, especially the things you used to enjoy before the compulsive behavior took over.

Patients often ask, "Why is quitting better than cutting back?" My standard response to that is that cutting back seems to be harder than quitting, based on published research and my own experiences with patients, and may not give the brain the chance to reset reward pathways.

———

When should we begin our dopamine fast? To optimize our chances of success, we should choose a quit date in the near future and plan for it. Maybe choose a date that has special significance for you, like a birthday or anniversary. If you're quitting a social media app, let your social network know you'll be gone for a period of time and give them other ways to contact you. Talking to friends and loved ones will never be more important than it is when you're on your dopamine fast. Find ways to make a connection where the medium itself isn't triggering you to use more. For example, try to meet in person whenever possible, but if in-real-life is not an option, consider a non-image-based way of interacting, like an old-fashioned phone call without any flickering images. I find that just listening without looking allows my mind to settle and focus on the content of the communication. In instances where seeing the person on a digital device is important, then make sure you're not trying to multitask but instead really focusing on the person or people in front of you. You might accomplish this by sitting some distance away from the screen, closing other apps and windows, and trying to sync your breathing with the person you're talking to, and, hopefully, they will do the same.

Plan other healthy activities you can engage in, as you'll most likely find yourself with lots of time on your hands. We'll delve into this more later with lots of examples in the section on hormesis.

And remember, you will feel worse before you feel better. The first ten to fourteen days can be brutal. Most people experience significant psychological distress to varying degrees when stopping any substance or behavior, including anxiety, irritability, insomnia, restlessness, depression, and craving, which can manifest as our brains telling us all the reasons we should go back to using, even though we committed otherwise. In chapter 5, on mindfulness, we'll really drill down on the craving piece of it. Withdrawal, including when giving up addictive behaviors, is also often characterized by physical signs and symptoms. I've had patients talk about dizziness, headaches, stomach pains, body tingling, and more when giving up social media, video games, gambling, and other similar compulsions. Of course, withdrawal from drugs and alcohol each have their own classic physical symptom profile .

But be patient. The sun will come out again, and it's worth the wait.

You've probably thought of more than one substance or behavior that you'd like to change, but I suggest focusing on only the most problematic substance or behavior. By focusing on just one substance or behavior at a time, you can narrow your intention and optimize for success. Later, you can go back and do it again for another substance or behavior. Having said that, it sometimes makes sense to tackle multiple substances or behaviors at the same time, especially if one clearly leads to another, something I call the *Stepping-Stone Effect*. For example, I realized that listening to pop music, most of which is about romance, gave me visceral cravings for reading romance novels. So part of my journey of abstinence meant, at least initially, limiting my exposure to pop music. We'll explore triggers for cravings in depth when we talk about self-binding.

For now, in the table on page 70, write down the substance or behavior you're thinking of stopping and when a possible quit date might be, as well as how long you plan to stay quit. Also, anticipate some of the withdrawal symptoms you will likely experience in the first ten to fourteen days of the fast.

For example, I decided to do a dopamine fast from romance novels for four weeks, and I anticipated being bored, anxious, and unable to sleep. All the withdrawal symptoms I anticipated came to pass, but I was surprised by how severe they were, especially in the evenings when I would usually read and now wasn't. I had unlearned the art of putting myself to sleep without my compulsive behaviors.

INTERACTIVE EXERCISE:
Anticipating a Quit Date

(Example: Anna)

Substance or behavior	Anticipated quit date	Anticipated length of fast	Anticipated withdrawal symptoms
Romance novels	Monday, my birthday	4 weeks	Boredom, anxiety, insomnia

Riley decided to give up all forms of digital entertainment for four weeks and expected to feel "uncomfortable, with boredom, loneliness, and anxiety."

INTERACTIVE EXERCISE:

Anticipating a Quit Date

(Example: Riley)

Substance or behavior	Anticipated quit date	Anticipated length of fast	Anticipated withdrawal symptoms
Digital entertainment	August 16 (a month before the start of the new school semester)	4 weeks	Feeling uncomfortable, with boredom, loneliness, anxiety

Andy decided to abstain from "exercise except for walking and light biking" for thirty days. His specific commitment was to stay away from the gym and the exercise machines that caused his injuries. He anticipated "Mental/emotional distress of feeling like I need to do more or I'll get out of shape."

INTERACTIVE EXERCISE:

Anticipating a Quit Date

(Example: Andy)

Substance or behavior	Anticipated quit date	Anticipated length of fast	Anticipated withdrawal symptoms
Overexercising to the point of physical harm	December 18	30 days (abstain from all exercise except for walking and light biking)	Mental/emotional distress of feeling like I need to do more or I'll get out of shape

Now it's your turn. Use the interactive table below to plan your dopamine fast.

Anticipating a Quit Date

Substance or behavior	Anticipated quit date	Anticipated length of fast	Anticipated withdrawal symptoms

Self-Binding

What about some specific strategies we can deploy to optimize our chances of success?

First and foremost, it's important to acknowledge that we cannot rely on willpower alone. Willpower is not an infinite resource. It seems to wane through the course of the day, being at its lowest at the end of the day, and is often insufficient to help us resist our substance or behavior of choice once presented with it.

Furthermore, in our dopamine-overloaded world, we don't have to go looking for our drugs. They chase us down. Think of all the push notifications and other forms of marketing and promotion we're exposed to on any given day, egging us on to consume, consume, consume.

Self-binding is the art of creating literal and metacognitive barriers between ourselves and our drug of choice so that we're not constantly being triggered to use, and so we can press the pause button between desire and consumption.

The concept of self-binding is illustrated by Homer's Odysseus.

Odysseus was sailing home from the Trojan War with his crew when he needed to devise a method for resisting the Sirens, those half-woman, half-bird creatures whose enchanted song lured sailors to their death on the rocky cliffs of nearby islands. The only way for a sailor to pass the Sirens unharmed was by not hearing them sing. Odysseus ordered his crew to put beeswax in their ears to block their hearing. The beeswax is a form of self-binding.

For himself, he asked his crew to tie him to the mast of the sailing ship, binding him even tighter if he begged to be unfastened or tried to break loose. Odysseus wanted to hear the song so he could tell others about it later, but he didn't want to be lured to his death by it.

As this famous Greek myth illustrates, to resist temptation, we must appreciate our limitations of self-control and bind ourselves in advance. I've grouped self-binding into three broad strategies—*Chronology* (*Time*),

Geography (Space), and *Category (Meaning)*—but there are likely many more categories and many other ways of thinking of this concept. But let's start with these three.

———

Chronological self-binding is a way to leverage time to help ourselves abstain.

The dopamine fast is an example of using chronology to limit our consumption. In the dopamine fast, we commit to abstaining from our drug of choice for a set time period. Simply knowing that there's an end date makes it easier to commit.

Four weeks can seem like a long time, until you consider it in the larger scope of your life. Take some time to reflect on how long you've been engaging in this behavior, relative to the time you plan to fast. It's probably a small fraction of the overall time you've been doing the behavior. Look again at the Lifetime Dopamine Chart you filled out earlier in chapter 1 on *D* is for *data*. On the same chart, fill in the dates of your planned fast. Now look at that time span relative to the overall time you've been using your drug of choice and notice how short your planned fast is relative to your overall use.

———

Geographical self-binding literally creates space between us and our drug of choice. By increasing the distance we need to travel or the work we need to do to get our reward, we can reduce triggers to use and give ourselves that extra bit of time we need to remember our original intentions.

Here are some examples of geographic self-binding my patients have told me about:

"I unplugged my TV and put it in my closet."

"I banished my game console to the garage."

"I don't use credit cards. Only cash."

"I call hotels beforehand to ask them to remove the minibar and the television."

"I got rid of my Kindle and easy access to books."

"I deleted my Snapchat, Instagram, TikTok, Twitter, etc."

"I put my iPad in a safety deposit box at Bank of America."

"I had my partner set my Screen Time passcode so I can't override my time limits."

I am frequently challenged by compulsive email checking, something I justify to myself as necessary for work, but the extent of which is not justified by work demands. I interrupt actual work with email checking. In the interactive table below, I list three examples of geographical self-binding to help with this problem: (1) Close my email program entirely so checking email would require opening the program again, creating a time delay; (2) Get a second laptop without email access for work; and (3) Disconnect my computer from Wi-Fi so that I'm not transmitting or receiving.

INTERACTIVE EXERCISE:
Geographical Self-Binding
(Example: Anna)

Substance or behavior	Geographic barrier 1	Geographic barrier 2	Geographic barrier 3
Compulsive email checking that interferes with actual work	Close my email program entirely so checking email would require opening the program again, creating a time delay	Get a second laptop without email access for work	Disconnect my computer from Wi-Fi so I'm not transmitting or receiving

My patient Riley, working to limit digital entertainment, "bought a phone with a smaller screen," "only downloaded essential apps," and sometimes went out without their phone altogether.

INTERACTIVE EXERCISE:
Geographical Self-Binding
(Example: Riley)

Substance or behavior	Geographic barrier 1	Geographic barrier 2	Geographic barrier 3
Digital entertainment on my phone	I bought a phone with a smaller screen	Only downloaded essential apps	Went out without my phone

Andy, who was overexercising to the point of physical harm, quit his membership at the gym, which also meant avoiding "people with the same kind of extreme exercising mindset and habits." For the dopamine fast to be successful, it is often crucial to avoid the people who engage in the types of behaviors we're trying to stop. This can compound our grief in the early stages, as we mourn the loss of the relationships that were strengthened by shared use, as well as the loss of the substance or behavior itself. Sometimes contact with this social group can resume once the dopamine fast is over and we're more solid in our recovery.

INTERACTIVE EXERCISE:
Geographical Self-Binding

(Example: Andy)

Substance or behavior	Geographic barrier 1	Geographic barrier 2	Geographic barrier 3
Overexercising to the point of physical harm	I quit my membership to a gym full of people with the same kind of extreme exercising mindset and habits	Abstain from all exercise except walking and light biking	Meet girlfriend after exercising to hold self accountable to time limit

Now list some ways you might use geography to create distance between yourself and your particular dopamine chase.

INTERACTIVE EXERCISE:
Geographical Self-Binding

Substance or behavior	Geographic barrier 1	Geographic barrier 2	Geographic barrier 3

Categorical self-binding is a way of using meaning to limit our consumption—in other words, considering the purpose of using a specific substance or behavior, and asking ourselves how our use aligns with our goals and values.

This method is especially useful for cessation or avoidance of triggers. It's also useful for addictive thoughts and fantasies that live inside our brains and hence can't be geographically relocated.

As one patient with sex addiction told me, "The bar is inside my brain."

Borrowing from 12 Step groups, a good way to think about this is to imagine concentric circles like a bull's-eye representing behaviors you want to avoid and those you want to approach.

The center circle represents our drug of choice, which we plan to abstain from during the dopamine fast and with which we hope to have a healthier relationship going forward.

The second circle represents the substances or behaviors that we should avoid because they trigger us to want our drug of choice but don't represent the drug itself (see Pavlov's cue-dependent learning).

The third circle represents healthier coping strategies we can employ in the very moment we get cravings to use. These are the choices and behaviors that restore us without triggering. We want to be careful not to replace one high-dopamine reward with another, like replacing Netflix with cupcakes. First, this practice may interfere with our ability to reset reward pathways, which is key to the whole process of breaking the cycle of compulsive over-consumption. Second, this practice puts us at risk for getting addicted to the replacement reward, otherwise known as *cross-addiction*. This circle represents the kinds of behaviors we want more of in our lives: what we should be aiming for, not avoiding.

For instance, my patient Justin, briefly referenced at the beginning of the workbook who was compulsively consuming video games, put video games in the inner circle, YouTube videos of people playing video games in the second circle (because watching YouTube made him crave video games), and playing with his dog, going on walks, getting back to college, majoring in computer science, and dedicating himself to his studies in his outermost circle.

The Avoid Approach: Concentric Circles of Recovery

(Example: Justin)

For myself, I put compulsive, repetitive worries about my kids in my inner circle, googling or using the Internet to compulsively research these related worries in my middle circle, and spending time with my kids without trying to manage their lives in my outermost circle.

INTERACTIVE EXERCISE:

The Avoid Approach: Concentric Circles of Recovery

(Example: Anna)

Why not try this yourself? In the interactive exercise below, use the three circles to help conceptualize your own concentric circles of recovery.

INTERACTIVE EXERCISE:

The Avoid Approach: Concentric Circles of Recovery

_____

We will now narrow our focus on the second circle of the concentric circles of recovery. Take a moment to think deeply about those internal and external triggers of our compulsive behaviors. A successful dopamine fast must also include avoiding the people, places, and things that remind us of our drug of choice. These non-drug cues can release dopamine in our brain's reward pathway and thereby trigger the same cascade of desire, withdrawal, and craving as the drug itself. In the world of neuroscience, this is called *cue-dependent learning*, also known as *classical (Pavlovian) conditioning*.

Ivan Pavlov, who won the Nobel Prize in Physiology or Medicine in 1904, demonstrated that dogs reflexively salivate when presented with a slab of meat. When the presentation of meat is consistently paired with the sound of a buzzer, the dogs salivate when they hear the buzzer, even if no meat is immediately forthcoming. The interpretation is that the dogs have learned to associate the slab of meat, a natural reward, with the buzzer, a conditioned cue.

What's happening in the brain? By inserting a detection probe into a rat's brain, neuroscientists can demonstrate that dopamine is released not just in response to the drug but also in response to reminders, or cues, of the drug.

The image opposite shows how dopamine levels increase above baseline in a rat's brain when it sees a light that predicts the delivery of cocaine from a button press.

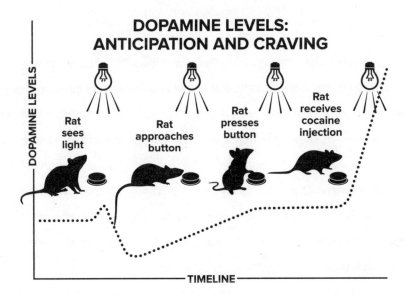

But look what happens after the rat sees the light. Dopamine levels decrease not just to baseline but below baseline. This mini dopamine-deficit state creates the craving and distress that motivates the rat to do the work to get the reward, in this case pressing the button for cocaine.

Of course, the cocaine itself causes a much larger rise in dopamine levels than the drug cue, but the key here is that the cue for the drug set off its own cycle of intoxication and withdrawal. My colleague Rob Malenka, a neuroscientist, once said to me that "the measure of how addicted a laboratory animal is comes down to how hard that animal is willing to work to obtain its drug—by pressing a button, navigating a maze, climbing up a chute." I've found the same to be true for humans.

In fact, some of the hardest-working humans I have ever met are people with addiction in pursuit of their drug. Not to mention that the entire cycle of anticipation and craving can occur outside the threshold of conscious awareness, making it that much harder to get a handle on.

What happens in a scenario in which the reward we anticipated doesn't materialize? The rat sees the light and presses the button for cocaine, but no cocaine is forthcoming. Bummer! In response to a reward that was expected but doesn't arrive, dopamine levels don't remain neutral. Instead, they fall well below baseline.

We've all experienced the letdown of unmet expectations. An expected reward that fails to materialize is worse than a reward that was never anticipated in the first place. That's because unmet expectations are associated with a profound dopamine deficit.

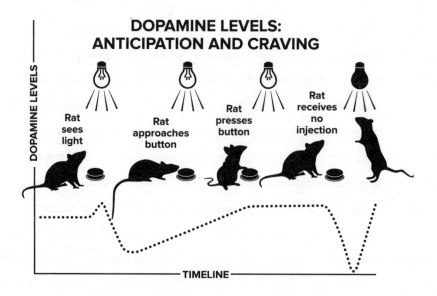

Sometimes this kind of disappointment is enough to discourage us from pursuing that substance or doing that activity again. But other times, an expected reward that fails to materialize can fuel continued drug seeking in an effort to re-create the original high.

This phenomenon is perhaps best illustrated by pathological gamblers.

Studies indicate that dopamine release as a result of pathological gambling links to the unpredictability of the reward delivery, rather than the final (often monetary) reward itself.

My patients with gambling addictions have told me that while they are gambling, a part of them *wants* to lose because losses justify continued play and induce a bigger high when they win. This phenomenon is called *loss chasing*. In a 2010 study, Jakob Linnet and colleagues measured the dopamine release in people addicted to gambling and healthy controls while winning and losing money. There were no distinct differences between the two groups when they won money. Both had an increase in reward dopamine. However, when pathological gamblers lost money, their brains showed a marked increase in dopamine firing compared to healthy controls. Pathological gamblers got the biggest hits of dopamine when the probability of losing and winning were identical (50 percent)—representing maximum uncertainty. It seems pathological gamblers felt good when they were winning money *and* when they were losing money, whereas healthy controls felt good only when they were winning money.

Pathological gamblers aren't addicted to money. They're addicted to the game.

Let's take some time to write down our own triggers. Just the practice of writing down the specific antecedents of the addictive pattern—what we're doing or thinking or feeling right before we use—without trying to change the behavior at all can be enlightening. In the table on page 88, identify an instance of the addictive pattern you're trying to change, and then reflect on what you were *doing, thinking,* and *feeling* right before you initiated the pattern.

For example, when I consider this exercise as it relates to my compulsive email checking, I note that I'm usually engaging in a challenging work task on my laptop when the urge arises to check my email. My thoughts are marked by frustration and uncertainty, that is, not knowing exactly how to go about the work task at hand. I'm feeling tired, overwhelmed, or frustrated, and want to escape these feelings.

INTERACTIVE EXERCISE:
Triggers for Addictive Patterns (Second Circle)

(Example: Anna)

Addictive patterns I want to change	Doing: What I am doing just before the addictive patterns happen	Thinking: What I am thinking just before the addictive patterns happen	Feeling: What I am feeling just before the addictive patterns happen
Compulsively checking my email many, many times throughout the day, beyond what is necessary or useful	Usually I am working on my laptop	I get to a point when I lose focus, get distracted, and/or am not quite sure what the next step is	I'm usually feeling tired, overwhelmed, or frustrated by all I have to do and want to reward myself. This often occurs before I've accomplished much or anything at all.

Andy is usually at the gym, at the middle to end of his workout, when he gets triggered to overexercise. He thinks, "If I do a little more, I'll get more muscular and lean and strong." What he feels is "discomfort—fear of feeling guilty afterward that I didn't try hard enough" and "skin crawling." The sense of "skin crawling" captures the powerful mind-body connection.

INTERACTIVE EXERCISE:
Triggers for Addictive Patterns (Second Circle)
(Example: Andy)

Addictive patterns I want to change	Doing: What I am doing just before the addictive patterns happen	Thinking: What I am thinking just before the addictive patterns happen	Feeling: What I am feeling just before the addictive patterns happen
Overdoing it with exercise	At the gym, about middle to end of workout	If I do a little more, I'll get more muscular and lean and strong	Discomfort—fear of feeling guilty afterward that I didn't try hard enough; skin crawling

How about you? What are you *doing, thinking,* and *feeling* when you get triggered to use the substance or engage in the behavior you're trying to fast from?

Triggers for Addictive Patterns (Second Circle)

Addictive patterns I want to change	Doing: What I am doing just before the addictive patterns happen	Thinking: What I am thinking just before the addictive patterns happen	Feeling: What I am feeling just before the addictive patterns happen

Relatedly, it can be helpful to make contingency plans around triggers in the form of if-then statements. For example, "If I'm at a party and somebody offers me wine, then I'll say, 'Thank you, but I'll stick to kombucha today.'" Or "If my screen-time limit pops up while I'm watching TikTok, then I'll put my phone down for at least five minutes before deciding if I want to continue watching." Anticipating and making a specific contingency plan for when those cues and seemingly irresistible urges arise can be helpful.

Patients will often ask me, "Can I use another reward to replace the reward I'm trying to give up?" like replacing cannabis with nicotine or cupcakes with social media. The danger here is cross-addiction, that is, replacing one addiction with another. Healthy adaptive replacement behavior is fine, like going on walks, reaching out to a friend, or doing a breathing exercise, but beware of other intoxicants.

In the interactive table on page 92, let's create three specific contingency plans for our triggers, using the if-then statements.

For myself, *if* I'm working and get bored, tired, frustrated, and want to reward myself (even though I often haven't done any work yet that needs rewarding), *then* I can: (1) let myself sit and rest for a few moments right where I am, breathing deeply in and out and looking out the window at nature and the sky; (2) grab a fidget toy and let my hands mindlessly stray for a few moments before coming back to the task at hand; or (3) get up off my chair and take myself into another room or outside and sit or walk in nature. Note how just slowing things down and putting a little pause between desire and action allows us to reconnect with our original intentions and escape the compulsive loop.

INTERACTIVE EXERCISE:

"If-Then" Trigger Behavior Contingency Plan

(Example: Anna)

Trigger	Contingency plan 1	Contingency plan 2	Contingency plan 3
If I'm working and get bored, tired, frustrated, and want to reward myself (even though I often haven't done any work yet that needs rewarding)	Then I'll just let myself sit and rest for a few moments right where I am, breathing deeply in and out and looking out the window at nature and the sky	Then I'll grab a fidget toy and let my hands mindlessly stray for a few moments before coming back to the task at hand	Then I'll get up off my chair and take myself into another room or outside and sit or walk in nature

Andy writes that if he has extra time at the end of a workout, when he might be vulnerable to overdoing it, then he could: (1) remind himself to stop after a predetermined number of sets of repetitions; (2) get water and think about "what I really want to do"; or (3) leave the gym and "call my mom, who is always up early." Again, Andy is wisely turning to other people to help create guardrails for his behavior.

"If-Then" Trigger Behavior Contingency Plan

(Example: Andy)

Trigger	Contingency plan 1	Contingency plan 2	Contingency plan 3
Have extra time at the end of a workout	Stop after predetermined # sets/reps	Go to the bathroom, get water, and think about what I really want to do	Leave the gym and call my mom, who is always up early

Now it's your turn. What are the if-then statements you can prepare in advance as a form of self-binding to manage triggers?

INTERACTIVE EXERCISE:

"If-Then" Trigger Behavior Contingency Plan

Trigger	Contingency plan 1	Contingency plan 2	Contingency plan 3

———

After focusing on the second circle involving triggers, let's now turn our attention to the outermost circle, where we list behaviors we want more of in our lives. This exercise reminds us to think about what to approach as well as what to avoid. Most of us can use our willpower to say no for a period of time, but what happens after that? It gets hard to keep saying no over and over again. It's also beneficial to focus on saying yes to being healthy and living in accordance with our values. It makes the encounters less warlike and turns them into positive experiences where we get to reaffirm our commitment to ourselves, our values, and our health. So in addition to creating barriers between ourselves and our drug, let's note the positive, healthy activities we want to engage in, and be specific about how those activities will or do align with our longer-term goals for health or achievement.

To do that, it might be helpful to spend a moment thinking about values. In the social sciences, values are beliefs that guide how we live, informed by what we think is meaningful and important. When it comes to day-to-day choices, values help guide what we will engage in and what we will abstain from.

In the interactive exercise on page 96, let's break down how our values relate to the substance or behavior we're working to change; how our consumption goes against our values, goals, or character traits we aspire to; and what specific actions we can take to live more in accordance with our values and goals.

One of my highest goals and values is to be a good wife and mother. To achieve that, I know I need to stop compulsively worrying about my kids. My continuing to engage in this behavior interferes with my ability to be present and provide the support they need. Stopping or reducing this behavior helps me live in accordance with my values by allowing me to be present for them in a way that is helpful rather than hurtful.

INTERACTIVE EXERCISE:
Values-Based Self-Binding
(Example: Anna)

Value	Substance or behavior I want to change	How continued use goes against my values	How stopping or reducing use helps me live in accordance with my values
Be a good wife and mother	Stop compulsively worrying about my kids	Interferes with my ability to be present and provide support to my kids	Would allow me to be present for them in a way that is helpful

My patient Andy is committed to the values of health, self-responsibility, and honesty. Compulsively overexercising goes against these values and worsens his health with physical injuries. It also leads to lying to cover up the amount and intensity of use. Stopping or reducing this behavior helps him live in accordance with his values because, in his own words, it would allow him to "stay healthy without injuries," "be honest and have integrity," and "be responsible for taking care of myself."

INTERACTIVE EXERCISE:

Values-Based Self-Binding

(Example: Andy)

Value	Substance or behavior I want to change	How continued use goes against my values	How stopping or reducing use helps me live in accordance with my values
Health and self-responsibility; honesty	Compulsively overexercising	Worsens health with physical injuries; leads to lying to cover up amount/intensity of use, both to loved ones and to coworkers and clients	Stay healthy without injuries; allows me to be honest and have integrity; allows me to be responsible for taking care of myself

How about you? How does trying to live according to your goals and values provide a form of self-binding?

Values-Based Self-Binding

Value	Substance or behavior I want to change	How continued use goes against my values	How stopping or reducing use helps me live in accordance with my values

---

Coinciding with values are our important relationships with other people.

We are social creatures, which means we are highly susceptible to the people around us, for good and for bad. It's difficult if not impossible to stop a behavior that everyone around us is doing. Likewise, initiating a new behavior that is not normative in our chosen tribe is doable for a limited time period but challenging to sustain over months to years.

So we need to be intentional about whom we affiliate with when we're trying to limit or stop compulsive overconsumption. In some instances, this means creating space between ourselves and certain others. In other instances, it means seeking people out, especially those who will support us in our project of dopamine fasting and/or moderation, or even try it with us.

Whether through accountability buddies we identify on our own or engagement in more formal mutual help groups like Alcoholics Anonymous, affiliating with others might just make the difference in this challenging modern project of healthy living in a dopamine-overloaded world.

Now that you've made a plan for quitting for a period of time, consider sharing your plan for a dopamine fast with a friend or accountability buddy, someone you trust. It might not feel easy to start the conversation. Sharing this information with other human beings can be hard. This stuff can be embarrassing.

I know that for me as a physician, disclosing my addiction to romance novels and eventually erotica was deeply shameful. As a recognized healer, I felt that I wasn't allowed to lack control around the ways I self-soothe, and that to admit these behaviors would undermine my professional identity.

But it was sharing my behaviors with a colleague that allowed me to do something about the behavior. Make a list of the names of one to three trusted individuals in your life whom you feel you could safely open up to about taking this step. You might even ask them to join you in going through this workbook, either to support you or to experience it with you.

Next to each name, list some of the feelings that come up for you when you imagine discussing your consumptive behaviors with someone else. Maybe it's fear of condemnation or abandonment? Although in my experience, when we share our failings with trusted others, they don't condemn or shun us. Instead, they love us more and feel closer to us for the telling.

My patient Riley noted that sharing struggles with a sponsor, "Sam," from 12 Step groups, or a friend, Jonah, brought up feelings of "shame/embarrassment about them seeing that I'm imperfect." Riley also noted feeling "scared they'll minimize it and think I'm overreacting." The fear of invalidation of our subjective experience is a common unseen driver of withholding our thoughts and feelings for fear people won't understand, or lying about our experiences to make them seem more legitimate in the eyes of others and ourselves. More on lying later.

Accountability Buddy

(Example: Riley)

Person I might confide in	Feelings that come up when I think about sharing
My sponsor, Sam My friend Jonah	Shame/embarrassment about them seeing that I'm "imperfect" and lack control. Or scared they'll minimize it and think I'm overreacting.

How about you? Who might you confide in, and what kinds of feelings arise when you think about revealing yourself to another human being?

Accountability Buddy

Person I might confide in	Feelings that come up when I think about sharing

Asceticism (aka Hormesis)

The A in DOPAMINE also stands for *asceticism*.

Asceticism is a word that means different things to different people. I use it here to refer to a lifestyle that intentionally seeks out difficult and even painful activities as a way of aligning our primitive wiring with our modern ecosystem. We are survivors. We're wired for struggle, especially of a physical nature. Yet we live in a world in which we're largely insulated from pain. And not just pain, but also discomfort of any kind. Everything is supplied to us at the touch of a finger. Now we struggle just to get up off the couch. Our modern ecosystem incentivizes inactivity. Inactivity breeds lethargy. Lethargy breeds anxiety and depression. We must fight against this.

It's quite a human accomplishment that the major perversion of modern wealthy societies is that we have to engineer our pain since we've eliminated its natural causes so thoroughly! But indeed we must.

It turns out that intentionally exposing ourselves to painful stimuli is a way to increase dopamine and other feel-good chemicals in our brain. Note here I'm not recommending self-harm or other extreme forms of pain. We're talking about right-size challenges that promote health, not detract from it.

Going back to our gremlins and our pleasure-pain balance, we learned that repeatedly pressing on the pleasure side of the balance leads to gremlins camped out on the pain side. Well, it turns out that pressing on the pain side of the balance causes the gremlins to hop on the pleasure side. We're getting our dopamine indirectly by paying for it up front and thereby avoiding the dopamine-deficit state that leads to anxiety, depression, and craving.

PLEASURE **PAIN**

This is the science of hormesis, which is Greek for "to set in motion." This branch of science has shown that exposing a living organism to mild to moderate doses of aversive stimuli increases transmission of feel-good neurotransmitters like dopamine, serotonin, norepinephrine, endogenous opioids, and endogenous cannabinoids. What we're doing when we expose our bodies to pain is setting in motion our own self-healing mechanisms. Examples include physical pain in the form of exercise, ice-cold water plunges, and intermittent fasting, as well as mental pain in the form of any mental activity that requires sustained concentration and/or tolerating discomfort, such as meditation, prayer, cognitive challenges, emotional challenges, creative endeavors, and so on.

While engaging in these kinds of painful activities, our dopamine levels rise slowly over the latter half of the activity and remain elevated for hours afterward before going back down to baseline, without ever going below baseline.

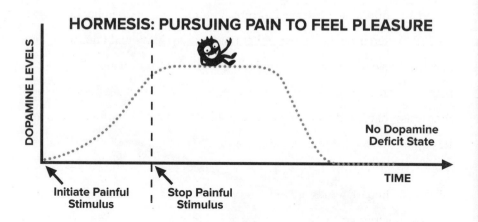

It's essential to anticipate our resistance to this activity. We have a keen memory for the initial stimuli of pleasure and pain, but not a very good memory for the gremlins that follow. When I pursue pleasure, it's hard to remember the pain that follows. Likewise, when I pursue pain, it's hard to remember the pleasure that follows.

When I first wake up in the morning, I literally can't remember how good I feel after exercising. I only remember that exercise hurts and I don't want to do it. So I have to find ways of reminding myself of the pleasure that follows pain. One way to do this is to write down how good we feel after doing something that is hard, and then keep that written reminder with us, for example on the nightstand, or pasted to our computers, or in a digital note on the desktop. We can concurrently remind ourselves of the despair, disappointment, and languishing feeling we get when we know we've avoided doing something that is good and healthy for us. You might think of this as a note to our future selves.

For example, here's a note I wrote to my future self:

> Dear Anna, tomorrow morning when you wake up it will be dark and you will NOT feel like getting out of bed. You'll think of a million reasons why it's really best if you stay right where you are. But I'm telling you, it's worth it. Get out of bed!! If you don't exercise, you'll feel grumpy and a little lost. You won't do it later in the day, even though you'll keep telling yourself you will. But if you do exercise, you'll feel happier, plus you'll get to watch the sunrise, your favorite time of day.

What note would you write to your future self?

INTERACTIVE EXERCISE:
Note to Future Self

_____

_____

_____

_____

_____

_____

_____

_____

_____

_____

_____

_____

There are many activites we might consider hormetic, that is, ways of leaning into pain to reset our reward pathways. Here's a list I've compiled based on my own experience and what my patients have told me over the years: making music; reading a hard book; talking to the barista, shopkeeper, or storekeeper instead of using the app; walking or biking instead of driving; writing a thank-you note; reaching out to old friends, parents, or grandparents; telling the truth; saying we're sorry; exercising in moderation (unplugged from a digital device); taking ice-cold water plunges; intermittent fasting; praying; meditating; cooking (unplugged); gardening (unplugged); caring for pets (unplugged); spending time with children (unplugged); being in nature (unplugged); cleaning out the closet (unplugged); washing the car (unplugged); and likely many more that you can think of.

Notice that some of these activities are not painful per se but are not always immediately gratifying, either. They often require sustained effort over time to lead to benefit. For example, prayer and meditation can sometimes be pleasurable but aren't predictably so. To experience their full benefit, we need to do them even if we don't necessarily feel like it. A patient who was struggling with alcohol told me that he learned he didn't need to feel like praying to get benefit from praying. *Good actions before good feelings* is a common theme in early recovery.

You'll also see that some of these activities are pretty ordinary everyday chores, but doing them "unplugged," without stimulating ourselves with digital media or music, might turn them into a challenge. In today's world, just sitting quietly without any external stimulus can feel effortful, precisely because we've gotten so used to priming our brains with high-reward sensory cues.

In the table below, circle the challenging (hormetic) activities you already do, or that you'd like to do more of, as a way to restore a healthier balance. Write in the hormetic activities that you could do that aren't listed.

INTERACTIVE EXERCISE:
Hormesis

(Circle the challenging activities that you already do or want to do going forward to reset reward pathways.)

Making music / playing an instrument	Reading a hard book	Talking to the barista, shopkeeper, or storekeeper instead of using the app	Walking or biking instead of driving
Writing a thank-you note	Reaching out to old friends, parents, grandparents	Telling the truth	Saying we're sorry
Exercising in moderation (unplugged)	Taking ice-cold water plunges	Intermittent fasting	Praying
Meditating	Cooking (unplugged)	Gardening (unplugged)	Caring for pets (unplugged)
Spending time with children (unplugged)	Being in nature (unplugged)	Cleaning out the closet (unplugged)	Washing the car (unplugged)

My patient Andy with the exercise addiction committed to "spending time with undivided attention" on his daughter on Wednesday evenings and every other weekend, when, according to his custody schedule, his daughter was with him. He reflected on the kinds of resistance his brain would generate just before this activity, which he described as "restless and anxious, thinking about loose ends at work, or ruminating about how to dig out from exercise addiction." This is interesting because it tells us that thinking about how to address his compulsive behaviors has become, to some extent, its own compulsion, and something he needs to work on letting go of. Having engaged in this effort at undivided attention on his daughter, Andy experienced feeling "happy and good about myself" and observed "how happy my daughter seems and looks with my increased engagement."

INTERACTIVE EXERCISE:

Tracking Subjective Well-Being Before and After Hormesis

(Example: Andy)

Challenging activity I can do instead of pursuing pleasure or as part of my overall wellness	When I might do this activity: what day of the week and what time of day	How I feel just before the activity: what I am thinking about	How I feel just after the activity: what I am thinking about	What I can do to remind myself that pleasure follows pain and to set up my life to make hormesis easier
Spending time with undivided attention on my daughter	Wednesday evenings and every other weekend (custody schedule)	Restless and anxious, thinking about loose ends at work or ruminating about how to dig out from exercise addiction	Feel happy and good about myself; think about how happy my daughter seems and looks with my increased engagement	Take a moment before picking up my daughter to remind myself that I feel better and more at peace by focusing on her and her interests when I'm with her rather than on me and my own concerns

And you? In the next interactive exercise, write down what and when you might do a challenging, hormetic activity, and consider doing it at the same time you would normally use your substance or behavior. So maybe instead of smoking in the evening, you could walk in the neighborhood, or read a challenging book, or call a friend, or take a cold shower. Describe briefly how you feel just before the activity, just after the activity, and what you can do to remind yourself that pleasure follows right-sized pain.

INTERACTIVE EXERCISE:

Tracking Subjective Well-Being Before and After Hormesis

Challenging activity I can do instead of pursuing pleasure or as part of my overall wellness	When I might do this activity: what day of the week and what time of day	How I feel just before the activity: what I am thinking about	How I feel just after the activity: what I am thinking about	What I can do to remind myself that pleasure follows pain and to set up my life to make hormesis easier

———

When it comes to challenging ourselves, especially with physically painful activities, we need to be careful that we don't overdo it. As mentioned previously, too much pain is not hormesis, and there's a real danger of getting addicted to pain, especially in today's druggified world where even healthy behaviors like exercise have been engineered to be addictive.

Examples of too much pain include cutting ourselves, overexercising, and highly restrictive dieting. Cutting leads to the release of endogenous opioids (the opioids our body makes), and therefore rapidly depletes our endogenous opioid system, requiring more frequent and deeper cuts over time to get the same effect. The result is long-term harm to the body. Too much exercise likewise exhausts the ability of the body to up-regulate feel-good neurotransmitters and instead leads to injury and overtraining syndrome. Pain stimuli that are too strong and/or too long-lasting don't lead to positive neuroadaptation. When we overload the balance on the pain side, we deplete our feel-good neurotransmitters and threaten to break the balance instead of making it more sensitive and resilient.

We also need to be wary of the *work hard–play hard* mentality, where we're pressing on the pain side all day long and then reward ourselves after a long and stressful day by pressing on the pleasure side, for example by drinking or overeating or bingeing on digital media. This pattern exhausts our pleasure-pain balance rather than helping us to be in balance.

Think about some days when you worked too hard or exposed yourself to too much stress, voluntarily or otherwise, only to find you came to the end of that day and couldn't relax or recover without overindulging in some kind of reward. This happens to me when I work too much and especially when I travel too much for work. I come home and overeat and watch hours of mindless YouTube to calm myself down. It feels like I can't do otherwise. The way to get out of this cycle is to try to reduce the stressor in the first place, to the extent we are able, so that stress doesn't create the craving to consume.

A rat in a cage that has learned to press a button for cocaine will press that button to exhaustion or until it dies. If the cocaine is taken away for a period of time long enough to extinguish that behavior, the rat will eventually stop pressing the button. But if the rat is then exposed to a very painful foot shock, the first thing it will do is run over to the button and start pressing it, looking for the cocaine it used to find there. In other words, stress causes us to reflexively return to compulsive behaviors we have used previously to access dopamine, even if those behaviors are self-destructive. The first step to preventing this kind of reflexive return to self-destructive behavior is, again, awareness. The second step is avoiding those kinds of stressors.

Since work travel is my big stressor, being judicious about when and how often I travel for work is key to achieving balance in my life.

INTERACTIVE EXERCISE:

Avoiding the Work Hard–Play Hard Trap

(Example: Anna)

Example of a stressor that will reflexively trigger compulsive overconsumption	Typical substance or behavior I use to try to restore homeostasis, i.e., stop feeling stressed	How I feel at the end of the work hard– play hard cycle	Some ways I might limit this particular type of stress in my life	Some ways I might cope wi stress better / m adaptively
Traveling for work, especially plane travel	Watching YouTube or sometimes TikTok	Worse. It doesn't work to relieve my stress. Makes me feel bad about myself.	Only travel if absolutely necessary	Exercise, talk wit family and friend sleep

In the next interactive exercise, think about a situation that creates stress-induced craving for you, the behavior you engage with in response to that stressor, and what you can do to try to reduce that kind of stress in your life, as well as develop healthier coping strategies when the stressor is unavoidable.

INTERACTIVE EXERCISE:

Avoiding the Work Hard–Play Hard Trap

Example of a stressor that will reflexively trigger compulsive overconsumption	Typical substance or behavior I use to try to restore homeostasis, i.e., stop feeling stressed	How I feel at the end of the work hard– play hard cycle	Some ways I might limit this particular type of stress in my life	Some ways I might cope with stress better / more adaptively

---

We've come to the end of the chapter on "A is for *abstinence and asceticism*." This was a long one, but you got through it. Nice work! Let's take a moment for a quick recap.

Recap

- We've planned for the dopamine fast, including what, when, and how long, with the recommendation being at least four weeks, while acknowledging this may not be possible for everyone.
- We've explored self-binding as a way to leverage willpower by creating literal and metacognitive barriers between ourselves and our drug of choice so we can press the pause button between desire and consumption.
- We've contemplated asceticism, or the science of hormesis, as a way to get our feel-good neurotransmitters like dopamine indirectly by paying for them up front, while remaining careful about not overdoing pain or getting addicted to pain.

———

Before going on to the next chapter, you should begin your dopamine fast. The exercises in chapters 5 and 6 are intended to be completed during the dopamine fast and especially in those first ten to fourteen days when withdrawal is at its peak.

CHAPTER 5

Mindfulness

 D = Data

O = Objectives

P = Problems

 = Abstinence and Asceticism

 = **Mindfulness**

= Insight (and Radical Honesty)

= Next Steps

 = Experiment

The *M* in DOPAMINE stands for *mindfulness*.

The exercises in this chapter should ideally be completed in the early stages of your dopamine fast.

Mindfulness is a word that gets used a lot these days without a whole lot of explanation of what it means. So let's define it.

Mindfulness is the act of observing our own thoughts and feelings with nonreactive curiosity and compassion and, equally important, without trying to escape those thoughts and feelings. It's a skill, which means the more we practice it, the better we get at it.

Unlike much of our other mental activity, in which thoughts and feelings occur spontaneously and sometimes outside of awareness, when we're being mindful, we are using our mind to watch our mind. By watching our own minds, we quickly come to several important conclusions.

First, our minds are busy. The flow of thoughts and emotions is like a rapidly flowing river. The ceaseless flow can be overwhelming.

Second, thoughts and emotions arise spontaneously without our willing them to happen, and sometimes what comes up is odd indeed. That's okay. Remember we're observing our minds without judgment.

Third, thoughts and feelings are fleeting and recurring, including negative thoughts. In the moment, negative thoughts can feel endless and overwhelming, but by preserving some degree of detachment, as the watcher, we can learn to tolerate them until they pass. This kind of patience and restraint, and trust that distressing thoughts and emotions are temporary, is key to engaging in the dopamine fast and abstaining from our drug of choice long enough to reset reward pathways.

Understanding the neuroscience of pleasure and pain, as discussed, can also help when we're practicing mindfulness by giving us a framework for knowing what is going on in our brains.

One reader told me how envisioning the gremlins jumping up and down on the pain side of the balance helped him quit smoking. "Every time I have a craving now," he said, "I just say to myself, 'Gremlins, other side!' It is silly, but it makes me smile. And it gives me a jolt of what I need to keep going."

PLEASURE   **PAIN**

As we go through the dopamine fast, especially those early weeks, we can use mindfulness practices to help us tolerate the universal symptoms of withdrawal: anxiety, irritability, insomnia, dysphoria, and craving.

As you enter into the first part of your dopamine fast, when withdrawal is at its peak, take some time to think about the messages your brain is sending you to rationalize ending the fast and using again. Our brains are amazing storytelling machines, and part of withdrawal is the elaborate tales our brains manufacture to persuade us to use again, against our intentions to abstain. One of the most common prompts simply invalidates the worthiness of the task itself, with messages like "This is stupid. Why are you even doing this?" or "This is a waste of your time and energy. There are many reasons why you should use again, right now." To counter these powerful voices in our heads, we have to remind ourselves of why we originally set forth on this road of fasting. Why it mattered to us, and what we hope to achieve.

Andy, who struggles with exercise addiction, described his voices of craving as follows: "Just twenty more minutes of exercise and two hundred fifty calories burned will give me relief and let me eat another bowl of oatmeal. Doesn't really matter, and I can get on a one-hour exercise-limit schedule later. Right now, I have the time and capability and don't want to deal with the distressing feelings of thinking I'm underdoing it. I need to feel like I can control my own body and emotions now." Note how his compulsive exercise is closely linked to his other compulsive behaviors, food restriction and calorie counting. Note too how much the exertion of personal control and the ability to change the way we feel *right now* is a potent aspect of any addiction.

Andy's counternarrative against the voices of craving is "If I continue to overexercise, my physical injuries will worsen. This is a mental illness that has become unmanageable and reliably leaves me feeling empty, anxious, and ashamed." Emphasizing the problematic nature of his behaviors in the long run helps remind Andy why he wants to resist the voices of craving.

INTERACTIVE EXERCISE:
Countering the Voices of Craving
(Example: Andy)

The voices of craving	Counternarratives to remind ourselves why abstaining is important
Just 20 more minutes of exercise and 250 calories burned will give me relief and let me eat another bowl of oatmeal. Doesn't really matter, and I can get on a one-hour exercise-limit schedule later. Right now, I have the time and capability and don't want to deal with the distressing feelings of thinking I'm underdoing it. I need to feel like I can control my own body and emotions now.	If I continue to overexercise, my physical injuries will worsen. This is a mental illness that has become unmanageable and reliably leaves me feeling empty, anxious, and ashamed.

In the interactive exercise below, write down the rationalizations your brain comes up with for stopping your fast, and then counter those narratives with the reasons it's important for you to finish what you set out to do. You might think of this as countering the voices of craving, which often manifest as perfectly rational voices telling us why it's okay to use again.

Countering the Voices of Craving

The voices of craving	Counternarratives to remind ourselves why abstaining is important

---

Before we end this section, a word on boredom. One of the mental states that it's important to recognize when we're trying to abstain from our drug of choice is boredom.

On the face of it, boredom seems a trivial emotion, but lurking beneath boredom is one of the most enduringly terrifying emotions of all time: the existential terror of being alive.

As long as we stay busy with our drug or otherwise, we don't have to look closely at the purpose of our existence. The whys and wherefores. Why we live and why we die. But in the absence of things to distract ourselves, boredom comes out roaring, and terror is not far behind. In my clinical experience, so-called boredom is among the most common reasons people give for relapse.

So we need to anticipate boredom, examine it closely, and, dare I say, welcome it. Boredom is an opportunity.

For one thing, boredom forces us to slow our lives down and just sit in the moment and wait for what comes next, something modern people are ill-equipped to do. Boredom also gives us the chance to reorder our lives and our priorities according to our goals and values. Further, boredom gives us the space and time we need for new ideas to be born. If necessity is the mother of invention, then boredom is its midwife.

We've come to the end of our chapter on "*M* is for *mindfulness*." Nice work! Let's take a moment for a quick recap.

Recap

- We've considered how busy our minds are and the importance of learning to sit and observe our thoughts and feelings without judging them or using a substance or behavior to get away from them. The only way we will come to know ourselves is to sit quietly with ourselves.
- We've explored the voices of craving, that is, the elaborate stories our brains make up in a nanosecond to get us to use, including telling us that the very project of abstinence is not worth the effort, even when we have many good reasons to fast. To counter these voices, we've created a counternarrative to remind ourselves of all the good reasons why we want and need to change our behavior.
- We've contemplated the problem of boredom during abstinence, a common reason for relapse, including the hidden meaning of boredom and how boredom can be a gateway to, and may even be necessary for, creativity.

We've practiced our mindfulness skills and are now ready for an advanced form of mindfulness—radical honesty. Most of us are such natural liars that even recognizing our everyday lies requires paying attention in a new way.

CHAPTER 6

Insight (and Radical Honesty)

 D = Data

O = Objectives

P = Problems

 A = Abstinence and Asceticism

M = Mindfulness

 I = **Insight (and Radical Honesty)**

N = Next Steps

E = Experiment

The *I* in DOPAMINE stands for *insight*.

Something very strange happens when we're chasing dopamine: We lose the ability to see true cause and effect.

Determining cause and effect in the world is hard anyway, as the world is a complex place with many forces working simultaneously to shape outcomes. It's hard to know what causes what, even when we're paying attention.

But when we're caught in the vortex of compulsive overconsumption, we are prone to overvalue our drug of choice and miss the signals that would warn us away. We're in a kind of waking dream, the realm of impulse and raw emotion.

The dopamine fast allows us the chance to escape the vortex of addiction for long enough to observe our behavior for what it is. My patients, once they've completed the fast, repeatedly express surprise at their using selves. They'll say things like the following: "I really thought the cannabis was helping my anxiety, but now I see it was making it worse." Or "Watching You-

Tube and TikTok seemed like a harmless way to spend time, but now I get how it was making me depressed." They're often devastated by how much time, energy, money, and creativity they put into getting, using, and hiding their addiction, time they now have for other, more productive goals.

———

In addition to the dopamine fast, how else can we optimize insight?

One of the daily practices I recommend to my patients, and try to incorporate in my own life as a tool for accelerating insight, is something I call *radical honesty*. I mentioned it briefly in chapter 4, but now we're going to delve into it.

Radical honesty is a commitment to telling the truth at all times, even about things that seem insignificant or inconsequential, with a special focus on avoiding lies that attempt to cover up our own mistakes and/or manipulate other people's impressions of us. The average adult tells one to two lies per day, so radical honesty is no small feat.

I say to patients, "In addition to stopping your drug of choice for four weeks, I'd like you to commit to telling no lies this month, not even about little things."

Maybe you haven't had interpersonal issues related to your use, or ruptures because of compulsive lying that gets wrapped up in your use. But for those who have, this chapter is especially important.

Radical honesty helps us curb compulsive overconsumption by working at many different levels in our brains. I briefly review four here: (1) Radical Honesty and the Prefrontal Cortex, (2) Radical Honesty and Intimacy,

(3) Radical Honesty and a Plenty Mindset, and (4) Radical Honesty and Pro-social Shame.

Radical Honesty and the Prefrontal Cortex

A patient of mine once told me that when he was deep in his addiction, he would lie about everything and didn't even know why. If he was getting lunch at Burger King and his friend called and said, "Where are you?" he would say, "McDonald's." If he was at McDonald's, he would say "Burger King." "It didn't make any sense," he said, "but I guess I got into the lying habit."

I am prone to lie about little things in order to make myself look less selfish or more important than I am. If I'm late for a meeting, I might say, "Sorry I'm late. Traffic was terrible," rather than simply "Sorry I'm late."

To manipulate others, I'm prone to exaggerate events to make me appear the victim; for example, I might say, "I was waiting for twenty minutes for him to arrive!" when in fact I was waiting only five.

By the way, I tell these lies largely outside of conscious awareness. I don't know I'm doing it. They're reflexive unless I'm really making an effort to tell the truth. Turns out I'm not alone.

The lying habit is remarkably easy for any of us to slip into, because telling the truth is hard, even when we're not addicted. We're wired to lie as a weapon and a shield, and language is our tool. The lying habit is even more common in addiction. You might say it's a nonspecific symptom of the disease. It starts with covering up our addictive behavior, but then comes to encompass everything we do.

Over many years of treating patients with addiction, I have observed that the patients who get into and maintain long-term recovery have made a commitment to telling the truth, even about trivial matters that seemed unrelated to addiction, and especially about their own shortcomings. Whether they quit on their own or through the help of a doctor, or get sober through Alcoholics Anonymous or other 12 Step groups, the practice of radical honesty is a recurring theme in recovery.

When we're telling the truth about our lives and also suffering the immediate consequences of our misdeeds, we become aware of our actions and the harm they cause others in a way that is simply not possible when we're lying. This increased access to more truthful information then translates into the way we tell our stories. (I say *more truthful* because we're all bounded by the human limit to know ultimate reality and also fallible in our capacity to see the truth even when it's in front of us.)

These self-stories, the autobiographical narratives of our lives, become not just a way to organize the past but also a way to navigate the future. Truthful narratives provide better road maps for good decision-making going forward. As discussed earlier, the prefrontal cortex, a part of our reward pathway, is involved in truth-telling.

Neuroscientist Christian Ruff and his colleagues have studied the neurobiology of honesty. In one experiment, they invited participants (145 total) to play a game in which they rolled dice for money, using a computer interface. Before each roll, a computer screen indicated which outcomes would yield the monetary payoff, up to 90 Swiss francs (about 100 US dollars).

Unlike gambling in a casino, participants could lie about the results of the dice roll to increase their winnings. The researchers were able to determine the degree of cheating by comparing the mean percentage of reported successful dice rolls against the 50 percent benchmark implied by fully honest reporting.

Not surprisingly, participants lied frequently. Compared with the 50 percent honesty benchmark, participants reported that 68 percent of their dice rolls had the desired outcome.

Then the researchers used electricity to enhance neuronal excitability in the participants' prefrontal brain cortices, with a tool called *transcranial direct current stimulation* (tDCS). The researchers found that lying went down by half when neural excitability in the prefrontal cortex went up. In addition, the increase in honesty "could not be explained by changes in material self-interest or moral beliefs and was dissociated from participants' impulsivity, willingness to take risks, and mood." They concluded that honesty can be strengthened by stimulating the prefrontal cortex, consistent with the idea that the "human brain has evolved mechanisms dedicated to control complex social behaviors."

I asked Christian Ruff, "If stimulating the prefrontal cortex causes people to be more honest, can being more honest stimulate the prefrontal cortex?" That is, might the practice of telling the truth strengthen activity and excitability in the parts of the brain we use for future planning, emotion regulation, and delayed gratification?

He responded, "Your question makes sense. I have no definitive answer to it, but I share your intuition that a dedicated neural process (like the prefrontal process involved in honesty) should be strengthened by repeated use. This is what happens during most types of learning; according to Donald Hebb's old mantra, *What fires together wires together.*"

Practicing radical honesty might strengthen dedicated neural circuits the same way that learning a second language, playing the piano, or mastering sudoku strengthens other circuits.

Consistent with the lived experience of people in recovery, radical honesty, or the truth-telling habit, may change the brain, allowing us to be more aware of our pleasure-pain balance and the mental processes driving compulsive overconsumption, and thereby overcoming it.

———

Using the interactive exercise on page 135, take a moment to recall any lies you've told in the last day, week, month. This should include the little lies you tell to cover up your own faults and mistakes. After thinking of an instance in which you lied, write it down, along with what thoughts and feelings motivated you to tell the lie.

Next, reflect on whether you thought the lie accomplished what you were hoping for, and, whether the impact was positive or negative, how it made you feel to see that response. Even when our lies accomplish what we had hoped, we can feel a kernel of shame taking seed.

Now think about what it would have felt like for you to tell the truth in that moment. The anticipation of admitting our wrongdoing is often accompanied by fear. The fear comes primarily from anticipating the negative consequences of our actions, especially the anticipated rejection of those we care about.

Finally, let's think about a time we told the truth about our misdeeds to the person we harmed, and how scary it was, and what happened afterward.

Hopefully, we'll be able to see in those reflections the different cycles of shame and how destructive shame compares and contrasts with prosocial shame.

For example, my patient Riley, who struggles with overconsuming digital entertainment, described an instance of lying as follows: "I told someone I was sleeping at someone's place nearby instead of saying I was taking a long bus ride home (late at night)." Already we can see that this lie seems unwarranted and unrelated to Riley's compulsive behavior, but we often lie when we don't need do, consistent with the lying habit. In thinking about what motivated this lie, Riley wrote, "I didn't want them to worry about me traveling late at night." Lying to take care of other people almost always involves some level of grandiosity, as if we knew what others' reactions might be to the truth.

After lying, Riley "felt I distanced myself from them because I didn't share with them what I was really doing." We almost universally put a wedge between ourselves and others and erode intimacy when we lie. This is the real cost of lying.

In thinking about what might have happened by telling the truth, Riley wrote, "They may have shared their concerns with me, but I could've shared why I felt it was safe." Riley has the insight to see that there was another, better way. If given the opportunity to do things differently, Riley said, "No, I wouldn't have done it again. The only thing I gained was that I was able to prevent them from feeling worried—and in this instance that wasn't my responsibility. And I would've rather fostered a more honest relationship with them. I went against my values."

INTERACTIVE EXERCISE:

Radical Honesty and the Prefrontal Cortex

(Example: Riley)

Instance of lying	What motivated me to tell the lie? Why did I do it?	What response did I get from lying?	What did I feel when I got that response?	What might have happened if I had told the truth instead?	Was the lie worth it? Given the opportunity to do it again, would I act differently? Why? Why not
I told someone I was sleeping at someone's place nearby instead of saying I was taking a long bus ride home (late at night).	I didn't want them to worry about me traveling late at night.	They didn't think anything of it—they didn't worry at all.	I felt I distanced myself from them because I didn't share with them what I was really doing.	They may have shared their concerns with me, but I could've shared why I felt it was safe.	No, I wouldn't have done it again. The only thing I gained was that was able to prevent them from feeling worried—and in this instance, that wasn't my responsibility. And I would've rather fostered a more honest relationship with them. I went against my values.

Take some time to think of an instance when you lied, why you did it, what response you got, what you felt when you got that response, what you think might have happened if you told the truth instead, and whether, given the opportunity to do it again, you would act differently.

INTERACTIVE EXERCISE:

Radical Honesty and the Prefrontal Cortex

Instance of lying	What motivated me to tell the lie? Why did I do it?	What response did I get from lying?	What did I feel when I got that response?	What might have happened if I had told the truth instead?	Was the lie worth it? Given the opportunity to do it again, would I act differently? Why? Why not?

Radical Honesty and Intimacy

One of the reasons we resist telling the truth is because we think that once people see our flaws, they'll go running. In fact, the opposite happens. When we open ourselves up to other people and make ourselves truly vulnerable, people come closer. I believe this is because they see in us their own flawed humanity and hence feel less alone.

Indeed, when we tell the truth, especially to those we've harmed, and they forgive us, we can experience an intimacy explosion, which by the way releases dopamine.

Oxytocin, a hormone much involved with falling in love, mother-child bonding, and lifetime-pair bonding of sexual mates, binds to receptors on the dopamine-secreting neurons in the brain's reward pathway and enhances the firing of the reward circuit. So when we're telling the truth and the person we're telling it to accepts us instead of rejecting us, we may well experience a burst of oxytocin release in our brains, which in turn leads to dopamine release in the reward pathway, and that feels good.

Radical Honesty and a Plenty Mindset

Truth-telling is contagious, and so is lying. When the people around us have made a commitment to telling the truth, we are more likely to tell the truth ourselves, and also are better able to delay reward consumption. To illustrate, let me tell you about the Stanford marshmallow experiment.

The Stanford marshmallow experiment was a series of studies led by psychologist Walter Mischel in the late 1960s at Stanford University to study delayed gratification.

Children between the ages of three and six were offered a choice of one small reward provided immediately (a marshmallow) or two small rewards (two marshmallows) if the child could wait for approximately fifteen minutes without eating the first marshmallow. The marshmallow was placed on a plate on a table in a room that was otherwise empty of distractions: no toys, no other children. During that time, the researcher left the room and then returned when the fifteen minutes were up.

The purpose of the study was to determine when delayed gratification develops in children, as well as what kinds of real-life outcomes are associated with the ability, or lack thereof, to delay gratification.

The researchers discovered that of approximately one hundred children, one-third made it long enough to get the second marshmallow. Age was a major determinant: the older the child, the more able to delay. But it wasn't just age, and researchers found in follow-up studies that children who were able to wait for the second marshmallow tended to have better SAT scores and better educational attainment, and were overall cognitively and socially better-adjusted adolescents.

In 2012, researchers at the University of Rochester altered the 1968 Stanford marshmallow experiment in one crucial way: One group of children experienced a broken promise before the marshmallow test was conducted. The researchers told all the children that if they wanted the researcher to return before the fifteen minutes was up, all they needed to do was ring the bell, which sat on the desk right next to the marshmallow.

For half of the kids, the researchers indeed returned if the child rang the bell. For the other half, they did not. The children in the former group, where the researcher came back, were willing to wait up to four times longer (twelve minutes) for a second marshmallow than the children in the broken-promise group, where the researchers did not return when the child rang the bell.

How can we understand this?

When the people around us are reliable and tell us the truth, including keeping promises they've made to us, we feel more confident about the world and our own future in it. We feel we can rely not just on them but also on the world to be an orderly, predictable, safe kind of place. Even in the midst of scarcity, we feel confident that things will turn out okay and we can wait for future rewards. This is a plenty mindset.

Conversely, when the people around us lie and don't keep their promises, we feel less confident about the future. The world becomes a dangerous place that can't be relied upon to be orderly, predictable, or safe, and we are prone to competitive survival mode in which we favor short-term gains over long-term ones, independent of actual material wealth. This is a scarcity mindset.

Radical Honesty and Prosocial Shame

Shame is a gut punch of an emotion that combines self-loathing with fear of abandonment. We'll go to great lengths to avoid shame, and this includes lying about what, how much, and how often we're consuming our drug of choice.

But when we lie to avoid feeling shame, we paradoxically add to our shame by lying. Being dishonest with other people tickles our conscience, even if we try to pretend otherwise. Shame about our consumption is now added to the shame of lying, a compounded shame that leads to isolation and promotes addictive behaviors.

This cycle of destructive shame perpetuates addiction, wherein our drug of choice becomes a way to mask our shame and comfort us in our isolation.

By contrast, if we tell the truth in a trusted community, then we create the opportunity for prosocial shame. Prosocial shame rests on the idea that shame can be a useful emotion, by alerting us to wrongdoing and deterring us from repeating the behaviors. Prosocial shame, however, requires two conditions: the practice of radical honesty and an embracing community in which a post-shame to-do list provides specific steps for making amends. In this kind of community, being truthful helps to metabolize that shame, promoting intimacy and a path forward. For example, in Alcoholics Anonymous and other 12 Step groups, working the steps is the path to changing behavior and making amends. Likewise, certain religious and spiritual traditions provide specific actions to take for behavior change and penitence.

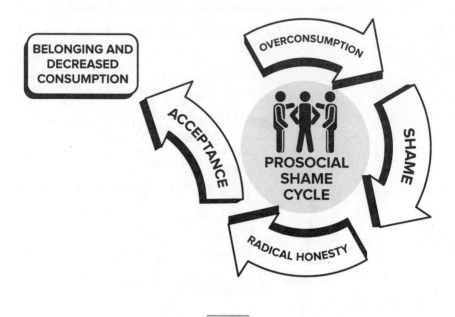

If this section on radical honesty was meaningful for you, I might suggest a more advanced version of this exercise adapted from the 12 Steps of Alcoholics Anonymous.

In AA, the "Step 4 Inventory" involves looking at past events and trying to be honest about the ways our own character defects, shortcomings, and fears have contributed to things going wrong in our lives, especially the ways we've harmed others, intentionally or not. You might think of this as *retrospective radical honesty*, that is, being radically honest about things that have already happened as a way to get clarity on them.

Start by writing down the people, places, and things you're mad at. List all the events you can think of that involved all the different people, places, and things until you've filled up the vertical column on the left-hand side of the table. Do this before moving on to the next column. Or alternatively, if you want to focus on just one person, place, thing, or event, that's okay too. You can always go back later and do the exercise again. Either way, no need to be too descriptive. Just jot it down.

In the next column, write down what that individual or entity did to you. Simply said, why are you mad at them? Maybe they insulted you. Maybe they owe you money. Maybe they broke a promise. Notice here how we're focusing first on anger toward others. This is important because anger is often the cover for shame, and it's the shame and self-loathing we need to get past to get better.

In the next column, write down how their actions affected you. What are the feelings behind the anger? A prominent theme here tends to be the ways in which our core identity is threatened, an ego bruise, so to speak. Maybe they made you feel imperfect, or defective, or unwanted.

Finally, write down what you did to contribute to the problem. What are your specific faults that made things worse? Examples might include that you weren't completely honest with them, or you didn't do all the things you promised you would do, or you had unrealistic expectations of them, or you didn't give them a way out. Maybe all you did was show up, in which case it really wasn't your fault in any way. But for most of us, there tends to be a theme that emerges around the ways we're protecting ourselves and failing to take responsibility for our actions.

The goal of this exercise is to look for themes that emerge that will help us understand ourselves better and, with that understanding, make better decisions going forward.

For example, Riley listed "my dad," "universities that didn't accept me," and "Rachel (a woman I had dated)" under "People, places, and things I am mad at." Riley's dad got mad at Riley during childhood for minor mistakes, the universities rejected Riley from their programs, and Riley's girlfriend decided to break up with Riley. The impact on Riley was a lifelong fear of making mistakes and seeming imperfect, resentment at not being able to attend the universities he wanted to, and a sense of shame that he felt unworthy in an important intimate relationship.

Now the hardest part—what Riley contributed to the problems. Riley wrote, "I was just being a kid who made an honest mistake—I don't think I contributed to the problem at that particular moment, but I ended up wanting to make my dad feel bad in revenge." With regard to the universities, Riley wrote, "I felt they wronged me by rejecting me—as if the only possible outcome was to rightfully accept me or wrongfully reject me." With respect to Rachel, Riley wrote, "I assumed that the only reason she would break up with me was because of some imperfection of mine. And I felt she wronged me because I assumed there couldn't be an imperfection within me that would lead her to the decision. I had a false, self-centered outlook."

After going through these reflections, Riley came to the following conclusion about personal character defects and maladaptive coping strategies: "I seem to have a self-centered outlook on things when the decisions other people make are not the decisions I want them to make. I often end up feeling anger toward such people. I usually end up wanting to make them feel bad in return, feel self-pity, or both."

INTERACTIVE EXERCISE:

Retrospective Radical Honesty

(Example: Riley)

People, places, and things I am mad at	What they did to me	How their actions affected me	What I contributed to the problem	Emerging themes about my character defects (the maladaptive ways I try to protect myself)
My dad	He expressed anger toward me when I made a mistake as a child.	I felt sad, unseen, and angry that I was yelled at for something I didn't do intentionally. I was scared to make mistakes in the future. I felt scared of being imperfect.	I was just being a kid who made an honest mistake—I don't think I contributed to the problem at that particular moment, but I ended up wanting to make my dad feel bad in revenge.	I seem to have a self-centered outlook on things when the decisions other people make are not the decisions I want them to make. I often end up feeling anger toward such people. I usually end up wanting to make them feel bad in return, feel self-pity, or both.
Universities that didn't accept me	They rejected me from going to their programs.	I wasn't able to learn in any of these institutions that I wanted to.	I felt they wronged me by rejecting me—as if the only possible outcome was to rightfully accept me or wrongfully reject me.	
Rachel (a woman I had dated)	She decided to break up with me.	I lost an intimate relationship with someone I cared for. I felt shame and sadness when she broke up with me because I felt I was too imperfect for her.	I assumed that the only reason she would break up with me was because of some imperfection of mine. And I felt she wronged me because I assumed there couldn't be an imperfection within me that would lead her to the decision. I had a false, self-centered outlook.	

In contrast to Riley, Andy decided to focus on just one instance of anger and resentment, his feelings toward his ex-wife. In reflecting on the source of his anger, Andy wrote, "She reneged on our 50/50 custody agreement to a 60/40 agreement," which affected him as follows: "Seeing myself as a 'good dad' was a core part of my identity, and her refusal of an equal custody split made me feel like a less worthy parent. Also, spending less time with my daughter made me feel sad about not seeing her."

In reflecting on what he had contributed to the problem, Andy wrote, "I initiated the divorce and my ex-wife was very angry about it. I also worked a lot during the marriage and could have been a more engaged, hands-on dad." At the end of the exercise, Andy was able to come to the following insights about his own character defects: "I blamed my ex-wife and got angry at her rather than owning how I could have been more focused and involved with our daughter during the marriage. I was concerned more about image to family and friends of less-than-equal custody split than the reality. My focus on my personal image over honesty is a character defect theme."

INTERACTIVE EXERCISE:

Retrospective Radical Honesty

(Example: Andy)

People, places, and things I am mad at	What they did to me	How their actions affected me	What I contributed to the problem	Emerging themes about my character defects (the maladaptive ways I try to protect myself)
My ex-wife	She reneged on our 50/50 custody agreement to a 60/40 agreement.	Seeing myself as a "good dad" was a core part of my identity, and her refusal of an equal custody split made me feel like a less worthy parent. Also, spending less time with my daughter made me feel sad about not seeing her.	I initiated the divorce and my ex-wife was very angry about it. I also worked a lot during the marriage and could have been a more engaged, hands-on dad.	I blamed my ex-wife and got angry at her rather than owning how I could have been more focused and involved with our daughter during the marriage. I was concerned more about image to family and friends of less-than-equal custody split than the reality. My focus on my personal image over honesty is a character-defect theme.

Now it's your turn. Think of the people, places, and/or things you feel anger or resentment toward and describe what was done to you that led to those feelings, how their actions affected you and your life, and what you may have contributed to the problem. Then review everything you've written and see if there are emerging themes about your character defects and the maladaptive ways you try to protect yourself during injury.

INTERACTIVE EXERCISE:

Retrospective Radical Honesty

People, places, and things I am mad at	What they did to me	How their actions affected me	What I contributed to the problem	Emerging themes about my character defects (the maladaptive ways I try to protect myself)

After decades of seeing patients and bearing witness to the impact of radical honesty on their lives, I've come to believe that radical honesty can help all of us decrease compulsive overconsumption in a dopamine-overloaded world and lead more balanced and fulfilling lives. I try to practice radical honesty in my own life—not that I'm always successful, indeed it's a daily struggle—but I find when I'm honest, my life goes better.

One final caveat about radical honesty: It's okay to refrain from telling the truth if to do so would be hurtful to others without achieving any other good. But be careful. We can often rationalize that continued lying is justified for this reason when it's not. Nonetheless, there are rare situations when it may make sense to tell a lie.

———

We've come to the end of our chapter on "*I* is for *insight*." Nice work! Let's take a moment for a quick recap.

Recap

- We've considered the lying habit as an integral part of compulsive overconsumption. The two tend to go hand in hand.
- We've explored radical honesty, actively telling the truth about all things whenever possible, as a practical tool for promoting insight, intimacy, a plenty mindset, and belonging, also known as *prosocial shame*.
- We've contemplated how radical honesty can also be applied to our past experience as a way to create more truthful autobiographical narratives of our lives, which in turn helps us understand our own character defects and how we contribute to our problems.

I recommend that you wait until you're almost done with your dopamine fast before going on to chapter 7. Or do a quick read through to the end of the workbook without doing the remaining exercises, then start your dopamine fast and come back to chapter 7 when your fast is nearly complete.

CHAPTER 7

Next Steps

= Data

= Objectives

= Problems

= Abstinence and Asceticism

= Mindfulness

= Insight (and Radical Honesty)

= **Next Steps**

= Experiment

The N and second-to-last letter in the DOPAMINE acronym stands for *next steps*.

You should be nearing the end of your dopamine fast when you begin this chapter, the purpose of which is to help you plan for what to do when the dopamine fast is over. So let's take stock and consider what comes next.

Begin with a pros and cons list. Write down all the things that were good about giving up your substance or behavior for a period of time. Write down all the things that were bad about it.

Andy had a long list of pros and a shorter list of cons, which is typically the case. On the pro side, Andy wrote: "Feeling better about myself with more time for relationships," "It's getting easier to be honest," "I have more time in general and am getting more done," "I feel less anxiety, guilt, and shame," "My body is less achy and tired," "It's easier to concentrate and I have more energy for hard, creative, intellectual work when I'm not so physically exhausted all the time," and "I feel a sense of hope that I can make changes and moderate and have my life work better, with more well-being and less suffering."

On the con side, Andy wrote: "I no longer go to the gym to work out with my friends there, and I miss seeing them and feeling a part of that group"; "Restless, agitated feelings that I could be in better shape"; and "I feel the burden of making choices to handle my time and emotions differently."

INTERACTIVE EXERCISE:

Pros and Cons of the Completed Dopamine Fast

(Example: Andy)

Pros of the dopamine fast	Cons of the dopamine fast
Feeling better about myself, with more time for relationships	I no longer go to the gym to work out with my friends there, and I miss seeing them and feeling a part of that group
It's getting easier to be honest	Restless, agitated feelings that I could be in better shape
I have more time in general and am getting more done	I feel the burden of making choices to handle my time and emotions differently
I feel less anxiety, guilt, and shame	
My body is less achy and tired	
It's easier to concentrate and I have more energy for hard, creative, intellectual work when I'm not so physically exhausted all the time	
I feel a sense of hope that I can make changes and moderate and have my life work better, with more well-being and less suffering	

Try putting this into practice yourself. List your pros and cons of the completed dopamine fast.

INTERACTIVE EXERCISE:

Pros and Cons of the Completed Dopamine Fast

Pros of the dopamine fast	Cons of the dopamine fast

In my clinical experience, about 80 percent of patients who successfully complete the dopamine fast will endorse more pros than cons. Among those 80 percent who endorse more benefit, including some with total resolution of the symptoms that brought them to the clinic in the first place, most of them will want to go back to using their substance or behavior of choice, but they want to use differently; they want to use less. And in most cases, they do end up using less, at least for a period of time. In short, they want to establish a healthier relationship with the substance or behavior. The other 20 percent will not feel better, in which case it's time to consider other causal factors, such as co-occurring mental illness, ongoing trauma/stress, etc.

Whether the goal is moderation or continued abstinence, it's important to write down a specific plan for use going forward—how much, when, and in what circumstances, as well as red flag indicators for when we're straying from that plan, and self-binding strategies that will help us reduce triggers for consumption.

My patient, Justin, introduced at the very beginning of this workbook, who abstained from video games for a month, felt vastly better for it. No longer suicidal and much less anxious, he found himself enjoying small pleasures again, like hanging out with friends and family, reading, and playing fetch with his dog.

He decided to continue to abstain for another three months to solidify those gains, but eventually he wanted to go back to playing video games, so together we made a plan.

First, he restricted his video game time to no more than two days a week, no more than two hours a day. That way, he left enough time between for the gremlins to hop off and for balance to be restored.

He avoided video games that were too potent . . . the ones that once he started, he couldn't stop. That way, he avoided accumulating more gremlins on his balance at once than he could handle.

Justin designated one laptop for gaming and a different one for school-work to maintain a physical separation between gaming and classwork.

Finally, he committed to playing only with friends, never with strangers, so that gaming strengthened his social connections. As described, human connection itself is a potent and adaptive source of dopamine.

How about you? How will you continue to abstain? Or if your goal is moderation, how will you integrate your substance or behavior of choice back into your life in a way that maintains healthy limits? What will you use? How much? How often? In what circumstances? What will be some warning signs that you're getting off track? What self-binding strategies can you leverage to optimize success?

INTERACTIVE EXERCISE:

Future Plans for Use

Drug	How much (time-based for process addictions, like video games)	How often	In what circumstance	Warning signs	Self-binding strategies

———

We've come to the end of our chapter on "*N* is for *next steps*." Nice work! Let's take a moment for a quick recap.

Recap

- We've considered the pros and cons of the dopamine fast. Hopefully, the pros have outweighed the cons, but if not, that's useful information as well.
- We've explored what we want to do now that the dopamine fast is over: whether we want to continue to abstain or go back to using in more moderation. Whatever we decide about next steps, we've made a detailed plan for what abstinence or moderation will look like, including warning signs for relapse and self-binding strategies to optimize for success.

———

Next is the final chapter of the workbook, where we take the specific plan we've made and try it out in the world and see how we do. No shame, no blame. It's all just more data from which to learn.

CHAPTER 8

Experiment

 D = Data

 O = Objectives

P = Problems

 A = Abstinence and Asceticism

 M = Mindfulness

 I = Insight (and Radical Honesty)

 N = Next Steps

 E = Experiment

The *E* and final letter in the DOPAMINE acronym stands for *experiment.*

After creating a specific plan for moderation or abstinence, whatever our goal may be, it's time to go back out into the world and see what happens. Some of us will be able to stick to the plan. Others will relapse right away and use even more than we were using before giving it up, sometimes called the *abstinence violation effect.*

Most of us will end up somewhere in between, with good days and bad days, requiring continual tweaking of our self-binding strategies and radical honesty to remain accountable to ourselves and others.

For myself, I took my patient's lead. I still watch YouTube videos, but I try to limit myself to no more than two days a week, no more than two hours a day, and preferably with friends and family. I avoid certain types of videos altogether, especially the ones that feel good in the moment but make me feel worse afterward. I try not to watch late at night, when my willpower to moderate is at its lowest. Instead, I try to find books to read, while avoiding romance novels altogether since they tend to leave me feeling worse than when

I started. Overall, the balance feels about right most of the time, although I will admit it takes constant effort and upkeep. I talked about the balance like a teeter-totter in a kids' playground, but it's really something closer to balancing a beam on a ball, like a circus act, requiring constant small micro-adjustments in footwork and body position to prevent falling off.

In the next and final interactive exercise, list the strategies you've been using to manage your compulsive overconsumption, including what has been working, what hasn't, and one or two small changes you can make today to improve things going forward.

What Is Working, What Isn't, and One Small Change You Can Make

What is working	What is not working	What I can augment or change

You've made your way through this workbook. Never give up. Practice, not perfection. Just keep on keeping on, and remember the DOPAMINE acronym and the Lessons of the Balance, and if and when you fall, just come back and try again.

D = Data

O = Objectives

P = Problems

A = Abstinence and Asceticism

M = Mindfulness

I = Insight (and Radical Honesty)

N = Next Steps

E = Experiment

Recap: The Lessons of the Balance

- The relentless pursuit of pleasure (and avoidance of pain) leads to pain.
- Recovery begins with abstinence (the dopamine fast).
- Abstinence resets the brain's reward pathway and with it our capacity to take joy in simpler pleasures.
- Self-binding creates literal and metacognitive space between desire and consumption, a modern necessity in our dopamine-overloaded world.
- Medications can help restore homeostasis, but consider what we lose by medicating away our pain (as I discuss in the book, *Dopamine Nation*).
- Pressing on the pain side resets our balance to the side of pleasure.
- Beware of getting addicted to pain.
- Radical honesty promotes awareness, enhances intimacy, and fosters a plenty mindset.
- Prosocial shame affirms that we belong to the human tribe.
- Instead of running away from the world, we can find escape by immersing ourselves in it.

ACKNOWLEDGMENTS

Many people contributed to the creation of this workbook, including readers of *Dopamine Nation* who wrote to me asking me for an interactive workbook to augment the ideas they explored in *Dopamine Nation*. Without your insistence, I doubt I would have found the time or motivation. Thank you. My gratitude goes to Steve Bachelder, Steven Michael Crane, E. J. Iannelli, Rod Jeppsen, Zach Katz, Joe Polish, Colonel Scott Reed, and Lieutenant Commander Stephen E. Rodriguez for reading the manuscript as it evolved and giving suggestions and critiques. The workbook is much better for it. I'm indebted to my agent, Bonnie Solow; my editors at Dutton, Stephen Morrow and Jill Schwartzman; and the entire Dutton team for their contributions and support of the broader *Dopamine Nation* project. Special thanks to Deb McCarroll for the original art in *Dopamine Nation*, and Soo Jin Ahn from the Korea team, and Paul Girard for adapting that art to the workbook. Finally, thanks to the many patients and readers who allowed me to use their process of recovery to illustrate these ideas. You are my heroes.

ABOUT THE AUTHOR

Anna Lembke is the medical director of Stanford Addiction Medicine, program director for the Stanford Addiction Medicine Fellowship, and chief of the Stanford Addiction Medicine Dual Diagnosis Clinic. She is the recipient of numerous awards for outstanding research in mental illness, for excellence in teaching, and for clinical innovation in treatment. A clinician scholar, she has published more than a hundred peer-reviewed papers, book chapters, and commentaries in prestigious outlets such as *The New England Journal of Medicine* and *The Journal of the American Medical Association*, as well as two bestselling books. She has been in leadership roles for several state and national addiction-focused organizations, has testified before various committees in the United States House of Representatives and Senate, keeps an active speaking calendar, and maintains a thriving clinical practice.